This is Your Time, Rwanda

The Emerging Story of a Bold Nation and its Brilliant Destiny

By Justine Rukeba Mbabazi, Esq.

© 2012

Justine Rukeba Mbabazi, Esq.
This Is Your Time, Rwanda. The Emerging Story of a Bold Nation and
its Brilliant Destiny
By Justine Rukeba Mbabazi, Esq.

ISBN: for paperback = 978-0-9852812-0-5
        for hardcover = 978-0-9852812-1-2

    1. Nonfiction. 2. Inspiration. 3. Historical non fiction

Printed in the USA.

Dedication

I hereby dedicate this book to all Rwandans who sacrificed their lives for the good of the nation, and to the late Major General Fred Gisa Rwigema—you are Rwanda's undisputed hero. A peaceful nation is what you died for. We are forever indebted to your selflessness and bravery.

To the late Vianny Rukeba: your wisdom and determination encouraged us to keep our promise!

I dedicate the book to my family: your love and support have kept me dreaming even bigger. I also would like to dedicate this book to my children, who have grown up to be my bestfriends. Thank you for inspiring me to write this book.

And finally, this is dedicated to the memory of my mother— who passed on her passion for hard work, love of education, and extraordinary devotion for our motherland to us. Her kindness, wisdom, and humility will be missed...for always.

Acknowledgments

I am extremely grateful to all people who spent their time reflecting with me on our history, and on our present and future aspirations. My heartfelt thanks go to the individuals who sent me testimonials on their dreams and admirations of Rwanda.

I specifically thank the Government officials, the Rwandan Association of University Women (RAUW members), the Diaspora Team, the Next Generation Connect (NGC Team), the Friends of Rwanda, and all family and friends who contributed to the section on 'Dreams and Admirations.' We all share a common commitment to the love of Rwanda.

Also, I must give special thanks to my friends, for their continued love and long-lasting belief in me. I hope you will read this book and be inspired. And finally, I would like to give special thanks to Linda Leon and Karen Cole for their tireless efforts in helping me to accomplish my dream of publishing a book. Their labors of love are extremely appreciated.

Table of Contents

FOREWORD

I met Justine Rukeba Mbabazi about fourteen years ago when I participated in an effort to bring her five children to Canada and reunite the family. Justine is a remarkable woman who arrived in Canada after the genocide with nothing. While supporting her family and ensuring her children received the best education possible, she also earned a law degree and then went back to Rwanda to use her training to help the country introduce laws and practices to ensure gender equality and opportunity for women. Rwanda ranks first globally in political participation for women, facilitated by low fertility rates for girls aged 15–19, and tremendous strides in reducing the gender pay gap. Justine is a leader in the effort to make sure that genocide does not define Rwandans. Instead, Justine celebrates the patriotism and heroism of ordinary citizens and encourages Rwandans to express and live their dreams for a better future.

Thus, in this volume, Justine's story is relegated to the margins. Instead, she has chosen to focus on the Rwandan people. In that focus, she has eulogized a number of other women who have played a prominent role in the resurrection of Rwanda—Veneranda Nzambazamaria, Judith Kanakuze, Jeanne Kadalika, Raika Felicite Umutanguha, the singer and songwriter, Kamaliza, and also paid tribute to the Rwandan women who continue to provide leadership: The Hon. Aloisea Inyumba, Minster of Gender and Family Affairs, The Hon. Speaker Rose Mukantabana, the parliamentarians Constance Mukayuhi Rwaka and Connie Bwiza Sekamana, Ambassador Solina Nyirahabimana, Ms. Marie-Claire Mukasine, Ms.

Zainabu Kayitesi, as well as other civil society activists, such as Godereva Mukasarasi, Immaculée Habiyambere, Immaculée Mukankubito, Suzanne Ruboneka, Esther Mujawayo, Jeanne d'Arc Kanakuze, and Ingabire Marie-Immaculée.

This is a love story. It is also a story of national rebirth in which "the spirit of our nation is destined to be victorious." The story that begins with atrocities, rape, and the murder of a million people in a hundred days is a narrative of a phoenix that have arisen from the ashes of civil war, genocide, and destruction, a romance based on deep love for the Rwandan people who now, evidently, not only believe in each other but "trust the Government to protect them and to do what is in their best interests" "to ensure that the corruption of prior generations would no longer be tolerated." This is in dramatic contrast with western societies where rights are primarily designed to protect individuals from the excesses of government power.

The story is also a familiar trope, though perhaps one more poignant than any of the others because it starts both with the fastest genocide in contemporary history and one that occurred even though the United Nations had peacekeeping troops in the country. Justine accuses the international community of actions "tantamount to treason". In contrast, the Rwandan people are resilient, honest, brilliant and beautiful, full of joy, enthusiasm, and self-confidence. The government both nurtures and reciprocates that love by allowing the people at the local level to forge and administer the laws of the country, most importantly in the Gacaca trials of the genocidaires, who were mostly tried at the local community level based on dialogue, confession, and reconciliation where most who were guilty of relatively small involvement were given only token punishment. The people have even forgiven the international community. According to Justine, all of this would not have been possible without the wise leadership of President Paul Kagame. As a result, the people have been unified not only in pursuing idealistic and non-selfish goals but in denouncing those pursuing self-interest and divisive ideas and activities.

Together, the sacrifices and selflessness of the people and the respect of the leadership for their dignity, history, sacrifices, and struggle have, according to Justine, not only restored peace and prosperity through reconciliation but have "made Rwanda into a paradise in a very short time" even though the genocide traumatized people for life. Rwanda is "unstoppable". This idyllic era purportedly resembles the pre-genocide period when Tutsis once regarded their Hutu neighbors as good and trusted friends, especially prior to 1959 when "Rwandans were all one people" and the "country was beautiful and progressing." The pre-independence period of Tutsi rule when "people lived mostly in harmony" and "were all one people" supposedly possessed the same romantic enchantment as the present in spite of the colonial efforts to exploit, divide and rule and initiate actions "carried out against our people's will" "under the guise of Christianity."

The Hutu rule from 1959 to 1994 have inherited and made worse the colonial values and practices as evidenced by atrocities toward the people which have escalated with every passing decade. The story is one of lightness and sunshine versus increasing darkness without any grays, darkness that included the period when the previous Hutu president and military dictator, Juvenal Habyarimana, though he never introduced equality of opportunity nor allowed the Tutsi refugees to return, initially ended the persecution of Tutsis when he first came to power. Salvation from 35 years of the dark ages ended when the Tutsi refugees under the leadership of the Rwandan Patriotic Front (RPF) liberated Rwanda and saved "the innocent people that were being killed by the corrupt regime." The current armed forces and national police, by contrast, support the community in their socio-economic activities and help build schools and participate in infrastructure projects. We in the West find it strange and worrisome to define the duty of the military "to enforce laws and policies in place to protect their people" except when we, as Rwanda also now does, send our soldiers abroad as peacekeepers.

Justice, reconciliation, and forgiveness are administered under the National Unity and Reconciliation Commission through *Umudugudu*, the local community process as well as through the following: *Umuganda*, public community voluntary service to contribute to the general well-being that predates the colonial period when it was used for exploitation; *Ubudehe*, voluntary work on behalf of the unfortunate, now expanded to include educational efforts for self-advancement; and *Imihigo*, the unique Rwandan system of accountability to and by the community. In order not "to lose the zeal of youth," these processes of community-rooted populist participatory democracy and "people power" are all inculcated in Itorero youth camps used to teach this story of Rwandan history. Itorero youth camps develop national unity and social solidarity as well as patriotism and integrity. The results are well established: "land sharing" and a new found food security, greatly improved health services, particularly with respect to countering the AIDS pandemic that has so ravished Africa, and enormous strides towards universal literacy and vast improvements in higher education. The achievement is a deep-seated patriotism and the foundation for hope and optimism where citizens strive to advance the good of all and not just their personal self-interests. These processes have an unacknowledged side benefit: the people are "so busy working that they are too tired and spent to allow these [ethnic] conflicts to have pre-eminence." Instead of "divide and rule", unity and self-determination (*maître chez nous*) become the foundation stones of society.

In this narrative, the constitution put in place in 2003 guarantees equity, the rule of law, the separation of powers, a pluralistic democratic system dedicated to the promotion of social welfare and justice and the "eradication of division"; that constitution promotes national unity through dialogue and consensus. These are not just dreamy ideals for, according to Justine, "Rwandan people are *doers*, not mere dreamers". Though guaranteed 30% of the parliamentary seats, in Rwanda, 56% of the legislature is made up of women; 30% of the cabinet and 70% of judges and magistrates are female because the women of Rwanda are "strong, determined and wise". Opportunities for higher education have proliferated. This romantic trope is not your traditional typical heroic communist tale. Entrepreneurship and private capital investment are all celebrated backed up by government provided laptops for every child as part of the effort to make Rwanda a leader in technology and communications. At the same time, self-interest is derided as Rwanda's unique path now offers a light unto the nations.

This is not a book of historical scholarship or of critical political science. It is a book about witnessing, about trust, faith and forgiveness that emerges from the Christian as well as socialist tradition of heroic nation building but now married to a faith in entrepreneurship and development. It was written with energy, enthusiasm, and clarity and is a perspective everyone, whatever are their views, should study and understand.

- Howard Adelman

Howard Adelman is Professor Emeritus of Philosophy at York University. His last two books published in 2011 were *No Return, No Refuge* co-authored with Elazar Barkan, by Columbia University Press, and *Reasonable Accommodation and Minority Cultures: Reflections on the Bouchard-Taylor Report* co-edited with Pierre Anctil, published by the University of Toronto Press. He has also written numerous other books and articles on refugees, genocide, and Rwanda, including the co-edited volume with Govind C. Rao (2003), *War and Peace in Zaire/Congo: Analyzing and Evaluating Intervention 1996-1997*, Africa World Press; the edited volume with Astri Suhrke (1999), *The Path of a Genocide: The Rwanda Crisis from Uganda to Zaire*, Transaction Books; and, most notably, the international study co-authored with Astri Suhrke (1996), *Early Warning and Conflict Management*, Volume 2 for the report, *The International Response to Conflict and Genocide: Lessons from the Rwanda Experience*, Copenhagen: Joint Evaluation of Emergency Assistance to Rwanda.

Preface

My children and I were sitting in a restaurant in Canada, specifically in Hamilton, Ontario. Looking me straight in the face, one of my daughters asked, "Mom, what makes Rwandans tick? Where do we get our self-confidence? It is not us alone—our friends from Rwanda are confident, too. Is this part of our blood?"

Just as proudly, my other daughter asked me, "Is there a place for us to read our stories?" I was speechless, knowing that in the back of my mind I had always wanted to write a book for our people, yet had made excuses, questioning my ability to write a book—or my not having enough time to finish one.

Continuing to encourage my children's dialog, I asked them why it was important to learn more about Rwanda. One of them said, "I guess we are curious because we want to be able to tell our children about our great heritage." But before I could speak, my other child asked, "Mom, why don't you write a book about Rwanda, especially since there are practically no books written in English about the country?"

I asked, "What would I write about?" They replied: "Write exactly what you tell us about Rwanda. Write about the work you always do, write about the resilience of our people, and your parents in the refugee camps. Write about what makes Rwanda so vast, deep, honest and beautiful."

My children's loving statements of courage brought tears to my eyes, and started me on an absolutely incredible journey. A few months after their challenging request, I found myself journaling the story of my people, enjoying the freedom to express myself in a way that Rwandans would be so very proud of. This would soon become a book sharing seventeen years of happiness and excitement about restoring our nation, and a way to tell the world about our new beginnings.

My zeal to complete this book was further fueled by my travels to Rwanda during the August 2010 presidential election. When I saw the joy and unity of our people during the presidential rally, it further confirmed to me that a book designed to capture the enthusiastic spirit of the common people and tell of their great works would bring even more excitement and inspiration to our blossoming new country of Rwanda!

When I arrived in the capital city Kigali on August 7, 2010 and traveled to a place called Bumbogo, I could feel great excitement in the air. I was surprised that Bumbogo still existed on the map—due to the horrible atrocities. A memory of my mother using a hymn book in which Bumbogo was sung about was the last time I remembered hearing the name. She used to sing that song whenever she missed her country, while living in a refugee settlement in Uganda.

To see that Bumbogo was still there was inspiring, far more so as I was amazed to see more than 150,000 people attending the rally. They were all dancing and chanting for one major goal: total peace in Rwanda. This was one of the most humbling experiences in my life. There was so much joy written on the people's faces.

The leading party's red, white, and blue flag filled the village. People were passing out free umbrellas, flags, caps, and tshirts. There was so much wonderful activity taking place! I was with a South African journalist at the time, and he was overwhelmed by our event, wondering if this extreme joy was normal for Rwandans. I really did not know what to say, having never experienced this for myself before.

It was a special outpouring of enthusiasm for where we had come from—since those dark days of the horrific genocide—and where we were today, under the wise leadership of President Kagame. The activities were peaceful, well-organized, and safe for all of the people. The military, ministers, the public, and the officials were all enjoying the day—together—side by side each other.

People gave truthful, heartfelt testimonies about President Kagame's regime, describing the restoration of peace, reconciliation, and allowing our country the opportunity to prosper. They thanked the Government for the new educational system as well as the new healthcare system that were recently instituted. Their well-intentioned praises were endless.

A few days later, we were at the polls. People were casting their votes in a manner so organized that I was proud of this event, having experienced first-hand how polling is often violent and politically catastrophic. My life in the refugee camps had shown me how political firestorms could erupt in minutes. I had worked in war zones—I know the dangers associated with voting. Yet, I was witnessing peace, and watching people cast their votes as they lined up in alphabetical order, with confidence that their needs would be addressed. This was most definitively now the new Rwanda!

Thinking about what I had witnessed at the rally and the polls brought my children's challenge back to mind. I realized this was a story that must be told. I realized I could no longer make any excuses. I realized that a nation of people that rarely heard anything good about themselves in the mainstream media and who always seemed to be remembered by genocide would tremendously benefit from the good news of Rwanda.

That's exactly what this book would intend to do. I realized this is our time to shine and that the people of this world need to know about the brilliant people of Rwanda, who have done amazing things—convincing myself that the new Rwanda is an inspirational hope for other nations!

The people of Rwanda, especially and our young generation, must be told about our dignity, history, values, and the struggles. We did what many would have considered impossible. We rebuilt our nation into a thriving, peaceful place. We used our knowledge of the past, our determination for a better future, and our courage and confidence to leave an outstanding legacy for our children.

This book will show how our ordinary citizens working together with our leaders have made Rwanda a paradise in a very short period of time. Everyone should be applauded for their magnificent, heroic, and patriotic efforts. Our nation should especially be applauded for putting the past behind us, and for its sacrifices and selflessness for the good of the country. This book will deeply revere those who were lost in the genocide. They will forever be in our hearts. Our restoring the country has honored them.

We could never have achieved our present peace and security without the sacrifices made by our parents, our families, and those who fought valiantly to liberate us. Our ancestors left us much in the ways of deep wisdom and capable practices to live by. All of these people and their ample contributions are honored within the pages of this book.

Finally, this book honors our national resilience, our passions, our values, and our dreams. Most of all, it seeks to encourage the young people to respect, honor, and develop the heritage that has been given to them. It challenges us all to dream big and do great things for our Motherland. All of us have worked very hard to create a country that loves its people, provides a safe environment, and nurtures development. We now have a new nation, one that will leave future generations the best world for their children.

However, by no means do I wish to imply that I have captured everything whatsoever that needs to be told about Rwanda and our wonderful people. My hope is that this book will inspire others to write on what they feel about our country, our people, our history, and our legacy. It also aims to inspire our nation to be the best we can absolutely be, so that we can ensure our future will continue in peace and prosperity.

Finally, I hope this book challenges people to dream big for our country, and to bring their big ideas to pass through hard work, dedication, and devotion—all in the name of our national development.

Justine Rukeba Mbabazi, Esq.

Section One:

Divided, Destroyed, Determined

Chapter One: Death of a Nation

APRIL 6, 1994—President Juvénal Habyarimana is murdered! His plane crash, as it falls onto the grounds of the presidential residence, hurls our nation into the deepest chasms of living hell—*genocide.*

It begins in a gut-sickening instant, hideous gunshots shattering life as we know it. This incident is the spark igniting a methodically planned and well-funded act of genocide, actually years in the making. But our national news has a different name for it: "Problem extermination".

Death marches like an evil specter slicing through our defenseless Rwanda, mercilessly lusting for anyone whatsoever of Tutsi blood! However, an uncaring international community blindly turns its back to a nation pleading for help, fueling the insurgency.

Thinking of the gruesome events in those months of genocide against the Tutsi people and their mournful aftermath, it's hard to believe that human beings could treat and degrade each other so extremely. Rwandans slaughtered their fellow citizens with machetes—while the whole world watched in a growing eerie silence. This was unlike the Holocaust, where Nazis killed Jews but not a single Jew killed another one. In our country, Rwandans were murdering other Rwandans—right and left.

Ours was an insane, perpetually increasing bloodbath—Hutus exterminating Tutsis, with some 1,000,000 people dead in a mere 100 days.

This is the reality of our past: stark terror and genocide.

Gangs of men violently descend upon families in the night. At gunpoint, a weeping mother, dragged from her house, is forced into naked lewdness in the sight of her children. Frozen in terror, they plead for her, only to be tied, gagged, and placed in the front row. Their tiny eyes, red-rimmed and fixed, abhor her desperate struggles as she is stripped down in utmost shame. Man after man after man brutally, shamelessly ravages her.

The violence escalates throughout the night. Some of these men she recognizes, not being able to comprehend why those she knew and grew up with were violently mounting her. Each unlawful entry robs her soul of worth, dignity, and value. Her family is traumatized for life. It seems like only yesterday that she was their happy neighbor and a good, contented friend.

Finally it is over, but she still draws sobbing breaths through her freely flowing tears. Dazed and writhing on the harsh ground, in direst pain, she reaches out to console her children, only to be kicked aside as one of her persecutors snatches and strips her twelve-year-old daughter.

No strength to move, no strength to cry. The frenzy begins anew. Frantic screams of her innocent child assail her ears like the pains of labor. She gags down bitter vomit, watching the assault. By morning, their assailants walk away arrogantly. There isn't much life left in the victims, but they are relieved to at least be alive. That is until dusk falls once more, when commotion thunders all around, and the women and girls are taken again, again and mercilessly raped again—night after wretched night.

For every woman's story like this in Rwanda, others were also brutally tortured until their deaths. They were raped in the country fields and city public squares in broad daylight as their sons, husbands, and fathers helplessly watched (before they too were gruesomely murdered). Even those seeking asylum in the refugee camps were plundered. According to statistics, over 500,000 women were raped during the genocide, and the UN report states that 250,000 were infected with HIV/AIDS—in any case, all of their scars were horrible, deep, and permanent.

More about what happened to us:

The militia is storming a village. There is nowhere to go. It is too late to run or hide. A mother scrambles to find a sharp knife. Handing it to her son, she orders him to stab her in the heart. Lost in unspoken tears, he hears thunderous ramming at their door.

"You must do this!" With all the strength he has, he lunges.

Falling to his knees in agony, he touches her for the last time. She is spared from any further torment; but moments later, a machete slashes her son's body. In shock, he feels himself hacked open. Blood, so much blood—he swiftly breathes his last breath. Truth be told, people paid bribes to get shot in the head, rather than be hacked to death.

A father braves the streets before dark, his hysterical family in tow. They are heading for the safest area that they can imagine—the house of God.

Other families are streaming in their direction, knowing that the priests will provide protection. Finally they arrive, and joy floods over them as they are warmly welcomed by the priests and a handful of nuns. Tonight, they will surely sleep in peace. Families kneel devoutly in prayer. No doubt they ardently thank God for arriving safely. Father kisses his children on their heads and squeezes his wife's hand, loving signs that they will be okay, as long as they remain there.

When they kneel to thank God for a safe passage, the doors slam and lock behind them. This is a good sign, for the doors are impenetrable. Yet from somewhere, gunshots erupt as the deadly militia fires upon them. Father shields his family with his body—but not for long, as the bullets riddle both him and all of those he wanted to keep safe. Many noble men died in such a manner, courageously protecting their families.

Crimson oozes across the floor. Life ebbs away. No one is safe. Even the church has been polluted by the bloody madness of genocide.

The air outside is thick with stench. Rotting bodies of men, women, and children float downriver, like so many small logs for processing in a timber mill. The streets are littered with thousands upon thousands of the dead, where vital roads once were. There are no people here, only corpses. All is ghastly. Where will they be buried—will there be any end?

Those left alive are like blood-encrusted zombies, badly battered and mangled. They survive in refugee camps, also hiding in pits and other unusual places. Daily, the sound of gunning down life echoes. In some families, there are no survivors, simply the ethnic cleansing of entire generations.

No Rwandan family was left untouched: my family, their families, no matter which family, whether rich or poor, young or old. Perhaps the most regrettable losses were Hutus having intermarriages with Tutsis. No longer was there any such peace. Were wives, now their husbands' enemies, tearing their children's lives apart? Some men murdered their lovers as an act of loyalty to the cause. Others took a bullet for the dictatorship. Homes and buildings were destroyed. Properties were seized. Our nation was utterly, totally decimated, to the point where hope was dead.

Then as quickly as it began, it was over. In July of 1994, as the new Government was installed, we would pass by the gory remains of the dead and see specter-like children clinging to the corpses of their mothers and fathers, crying and starving. Women that survived, several ladies that were raped, stepped through the gruesome fields and claimed those orphans, as many of them had lost their own children.

Some of them were even carrying new children, from the invaders' savagery. For a brief moment, I had a welcome glimpse that our nation would surely soon recover. These courageous, wonderful women, in the midst of the awful atrocities, desired to be mothers—they still wanted those children, even if their own were never found.

It was surreal, the landscape of something far worse than war. Some would return home. Others would return only to useless rubble. Still others would be traumatized, unable to return to where the atrocities had happened. However, it didn't matter; those brave women glowed with a basic strength that was beyond anything I could've imagined.

These images could make a fictional Hollywood horror script, with the severity of our genocide making the outside world question the realism of violence. The well-laid plans of those horrendous acts were years in the making, and executed with speed and precision. It's important for the reader to understand the context in which this violence was initiated, in order to appreciate where we are today. We're a country rising from our own ashes, claiming our deepest pride and utmost value, and I believe we have finally emerged as the best country on the African continent. We are indeed the inspirational hope of the other oppressed nations.

Dr. Martin Luther King, Jr. once said, "Silence is the worst enemy of a human being." Rwandans suffered greatly, horrendously and immensely; but for the most part we were silent as the dictatorship wrapped its death grip around our country. Instead, we lived with our pain and fear. We tolerated the wrongs and did not challenge them to accountability. We have paid dearly for our silence. Since we did not denounce the prior lethal actions, it paved the way for genocide. It is now our full responsibility as human beings to rise above our fear, and raise our voices against the wrongs.

Some background on Rwanda:

Prior to 1959, Rwandans were all one people. The country was beautiful, slowly progressing like other underdeveloped countries. Rwanda had existed under a Tutsi monarchy for generations. People lived mostly in harmony. All that changed, as Belgium and France began to set up their agenda to occupy Rwanda under the guise of Christianity.

In general, the monarchy was suspicious about colonial intentions. Our history tells us that Rwanda was the only country in the region that never had a slave trade, because its leadership cared about people. However, due to colonial control in this era, slavery, cheap labor, and other divisive acts were actually carried out against our people's will.

Over time the West's agenda took root, and the monarchy was eventually overthrown. Tutsis then became a threat in the colonial era. In order to eliminate this, Germany, Belgium, and France created myths against the Tutsis, using them as a scapegoat for the problems facing the Hutu population, therefore stirring animosity between the Tutsi and Hutu people.

They created a social class in which Hutus were underrepresented, though they claimed that Hutus were the majority. At the same time, they would send agents to cause Hutus to question why a minority group (the Tutsis) was in power. Another myth was that the Tutsis were not originally from Rwanda—this laid the groundwork for a Hutu revolution.

That very methodical process administered by the West proliferated in the schools and all walks of life, making it impossible for Rwandans to dwell peacefully together. It destroyed trust, fostering the false notion that Tutsis were superior to Hutus. Also, there was a great disparity between Tutsi and Hutu economic and educational development.

Belgian masterminds used these factors to suggest that if all of the Tutsis were eliminated, all problems in Rwanda would cease. For 40 years, they created seeds of hatred that vastly poisoned our country—in order to overthrow the monarchy and create a new republic. By 1959, the monarchy was overturned in a conflict started by no more than 60 Hutu youth. A number of them had been secretly trained and funded by the Belgians, resulting in the first Tutsi massacre of thousands of people.

The general population didn't know what was really happening. But as they became aware, many Tutsis fled the country, never expecting it would be 35 years before they could come back home. By the 1960s, the colonial period ended, and the Belgians left the Hutus in power. They (along with the French) continued to foster and fund the suppression of the Tutsi people. And so the unrest continued to escalate, well into the 1990s.

As refugees, the Tutsis who left the country never lost the desire to return to their homeland. During their years in exile, they created political parties at different times; the most effective one was the RPF. This group's aim was to secure their right to return, liberate their country, and save the innocent people that were being killed by the corrupt regime.

On October 1st of 1990, they accomplished this mission through a guerrilla liberation movement type of war. The French supported the Hutu regime to fight against their liberation struggle, staged by Tutsis in the Eastern part of the country; the French continued to publicly support the war with finances, troops, and weapons to the militia regime, from 1990 to 1994.

When Hutu President Habyarimana's plane was shot down near Kigali International Airport in April of 1994, years of political unrest ignited in one of the worst bloodbaths in global history. By July of 1994, the RPF captured Kigali and stopped the genocide, leading to the Government now jointly run by all Rwandans (not just Tutsis or Hutus).

Our horrible genocide will remain a historical, unimaginably dark moment in the past for Rwanda. But it will also be a brilliant laser of light cutting through the blackest midnight, signaling the birth of our brand-new nation. Now, seventeen long but fascinating years later, we Rwandans, as one people, thrive together, with well-intentioned pride as our heritage.

Chapter Two: Birth of a Nation

Rwanda hemorrhaged smaller wells of blood from 1959 until 1994, being under corrupt leadership and a system of impunity (freedom from punishment or consequences from wrong actions). The atrocities toward our people escalated with every decade. In order for Rwanda to rebuild, various communities constructed a legal governance system that protected the nation from corruption, denounced impunity, and brought about swift justice and accountability. The reform that has successfully occurred over the last seventeen years is outstanding, and unique to our nation's history.

Our present Government is a good system that starts with local governance and justice within communities, extending into the districts and provincial level with the same structure—and then to the country's capitol city. Specifically, justice is served from our local communities, cutting through all judicial stages—with proper access to justice—to the High Court, and finally to the Supreme Court. In today's Rwanda, a female heads the SC; this is a triumph of which we are extremely proud, in light of the atrocities women suffered during the genocide.

In Rwanda, justice is served from the prosecutor's office to the Ministry of Justice—and from the ordinary courts to the smallest villages. People pay for the actual crimes they commit. In our new legal system, your position, power, ties, or associations do not exempt you from the law and its system of punishment. Suspicious activities or open forms of corruption are exposed and dealt with immediately. The Rwandan

Government and the Rwandan people have no tolerance for impunity.

The punishment is now definitely just—inmates are not tortured. When they complete their incarceration term, they are brought back into the community, assisted, so that they can live a normal life. In dealing with crimes related to genocide, it has become critical to provide assistance to these inmates, because the nation has to be reconciled.

All communities have decided that the path for the healing of our nation must include forgiveness and bringing these criminals as much as possible into a normal state of life. In these efforts, the Rwandan population shines tremendously! Daily, our citizens display patriotism, sacrifice, and goodwill toward their neighbors, to bring wholeness to the country— despite the pain and personal losses.

Unity and reconstruction, however, have come at a high cost. It has demanded of our nation self-sacrifice, patience, the willingness to work with our Government—and the ultimate cost, learning to trust each other. No one in our nation will ever be able to forget what had happened, or who had caused our pain. But on the whole, our nation is committed to forgiveness, fully realizing that it is the only way to move forward. However, forgiveness does not excuse the wrongs that were done. Instead, it emotionally releases the perpetrators, so that true healing can begin. Rwandans are choosing to master the act of forgiveness as individuals and as a nation.

Forgiving also means that you have to forgive yourself. Some people might say, "How do you expect me to forgive after what has been done?" Or, "If I forgive the perpetrator, will it dishonor those who were lost?" Then others are so angry they say, "I will never forgive."

People must be willing to realize that unless you forgive, your own life will be destroyed by anger and bitterness. Those Rwandans who have learned to embrace forgiveness, in turn, have freed themselves, realizing that forgiveness helps you more than the person you have chosen to forgive. Reconciliation and forgiveness are the hardest processes to go through, but as a nation we have shown the world our resilience and spirit of forgiveness. What our nation has realized and gloriously displayed is that proper justice, reconciliation, and forgiveness all work together. In our unique situation, the healing of our nation has required all three of these parts working harmoniously together.

Our people knew exactly where to start healing. First, we overhauled the justice and governance system as discussed previously. Next, we returned to the ways of our fathers, which had kept our country genocide-free for centuries. We began to talk amongst ourselves, humbly seated in the open "green grass" with our neighbors and community members. An ancient system of dialog and dispute resolution used by our ancestors called "the Gacaca Court"—a community-based justice system inspired by our Rwandan traditions of justice— was reinstated. This was the best possible solution for faster justice, healing, and reconciliation.

I remember what my father told me about how Gacaca was used. The victim and the accused were required to walk the same path to the "green grass" spot—where the meeting would be held. My father put it this way: "traveling by road, sorry by the foot, during that very long journey reconciliation would often take place." The wisdom of Gacaca is ageless, and our generation found it powerful enough to resolve national problems in the aftermath of genocide.

In traditional Gacaca, the village chief would gather trusted members of the community and those of good reputation to help him to hear the case. The belief was that in the midst of many wise people, understanding would be increased, a non-partisan assessment would be made, and a fair and just resolution would be provided. Embracing a similar system after genocide, the cases in Rwanda were handled quickly and effectively.

We have found that since Gacaca was used historically for our nation that it is a perfect modern mechanism for the Rwandan Justice System, and so it has been legally approved under the legislative system—one minor difference being that in the present Gacaca, it is a panel of twelve wise men and women, lead by a chairperson.

Genocide in Rwanda was so different than the Holocaust and genocides in other parts of the world that there was no particular system of justice established that would work in our particular situation. This was a unique Rwandan problem, and it required a unique Rwandan solution. Citizens of our country thought highly of Gacaca as a means of resolution, ratifying it under the law. Having the system of Gacaca legally approved under legislative body gave it the power to enforce justice in the right way for our nation.

In addition to the stability that Gacaca brought to our country, an even greater feat was accomplished—allowing Rwanda to shine as a beacon of light on the world scene. Our country established a democracy that truly empowers the citizens. The demands of the citizens are "passed up" to higher Government officials to enforce, instead of being "passed down" to the people. What the people of Rwanda literally did was to give themselves a national voice, since they realized that keeping silent was one of the main causes that allowed genocide to take place.

Communities at all levels dialog together. It is an amazing process to watch, and one that I have never seen enacted by other countries. The process of governing starts at the community level, and then it continues to the sector level, followed by the district level and finally to the provincial level. Each level is empowered to resolve matters such as healthcare, justice, minor theft, crimes, issues of security, and eradicating poverty.

What makes this dialog unique is that it focuses on making sure that people in the communities truly know each other and understand the problems facing their community and their neighbors. The meetings, discussions, and all the governing activities, from the lower levels through the provincial levels, are to connect people in a unified manner—where there is one voice when laws are finally established.

The practice of literally knowing our neighbors is what actually builds trust in our communities. Silence and fear were the tools our former regimes used to destroy the nation. A free voice and ample trust are what we have chosen to use instead, to rebuild our lovely nation. We have learned from the high prices we paid through genocide, and will not walk that blood-soaked path again. The new Rwanda weaves trust throughout all of our communities like an elegant, broadly-threaded colorful tapestry. You won't find a community in Rwanda where the people living next to each other don't know their families by name, or do not know what's going on in their area.

This wonderful community level is known as Umudugudu. People participating at this level know at least 50% of their neighbors. So in a community of some 200 homes, the average person knows 100 of their neighbors. They actively dialog, bringing important matters before the group that need to be resolved. The concerns of these citizens are passed up to local leaders who volunteer to serve the community. The leaders meet, discuss and resolve the concerns, or pass them up to the next level. Everyone is interconnected. This system of governing has worked extremely well over the last seventeen years.

Our leaders and authorities are truly accountable to our citizens, because the citizens have established a clear way for their needs to be known, and have demanded through the Constitution what needs be addressed by those they have entrusted to leadership. The leaders have heard the clear voice of the people, and that is what now governs our Rwanda.

Chapter Three: Reforming the Nation

This platform of trust woven into our country has vast implications for the relationship between our citizens and the Government. While the Government trusts the voice of the people to establish which laws and ways of governance are enacted, the people trust the Government to protect them and to do what is in their best interests. The culmination of this process is that the people and the Government have begun to believe in each other. Through such belief, everyone is now working in the best interests of our country. This is patriotism in its purest, deepest form.

The proliferation of trust has challenged each citizen to work for the good of our country. This has caused our Government to value the input of its citizens, for when the authorities look for resources to help fix problems in the country, they first head to the citizens for support, instead of seeking outside aid from the international community.

When our citizens began to see that the new Government respects them and wants their input, they began to trust in their abilities more, which prompted them to become more involved. In essence, our country started a cycle of empowerment. The end result can be seen in every aspect of Rwandan life, from eradicating poverty to democratizing the nation, to gender equality, to economic equality, and to all throughout our educational system. The old system of doing things has been abolished, and the new Rwanda is a country to be reckoned with on a global scale.

All of this was neither easy nor simple to fully legally accomplish. In the immediate aftermath of the genocide, we realized that we had no legal basis for our country to function. Reforming our nation had to begin with the establishment of a new Constitution. This process began at the local level, where the voices of the people were heard.

I am happy to say that as a patriotic citizen, I took part in the formation of a great document—one which has transformed Rwanda for good. It took seven years of intense dialog and the exploration of various ways to govern the nation between the citizens and the leadership to construct this great tool of reformation. Our new Constitution was adopted in 2003.

The Government made sure to engage and educate our citizens on what the Constitution was, and what actual legal powers it held. This open dialog between leadership and the communities is what taught the people of Rwanda how to speak out. They could now discuss how to make sure that impunity never happened again, for they needed to ensure that equality and equity were enforced under the law, and that people who committed crimes would be fairly and humanely punished.

Many elements of good governance and human dignity were addressed throughout our organic laws. The leadership wrote our Constitution so that our greatest concerns were properly addressed, and so that legal reforms were instituted. The people knew from the beginning that the new Government set the foundation to protect them and their rights, and to ensure that the corruption of prior generations would no longer be tolerated.

I played a role in the Inheritance and Marital Property Law dialog processes, and was able to see first-hand how our new system was working. The talks and vital exchanges of viewpoints until the final laws were implemented were exhilarating! It was a joyful, incredible experience to be a part of such a valued history. Before the 1994 genocide, there were indeed laws in our system; but they never protected anyone—because of corruption. In 1999, we reformed the IMPL, which granted the right for women to inherit property equally with any male. Also, it makes it clear that polygamy is illegal in Rwanda.

Every citizen has the right to get involved and see their concerns being addressed to their benefit. Ordinary people are actively rebuilding and reshaping our nation, as a day-to-day ongoing process.

The adoption of our Constitution in 2003 was a major victory for our newly enabled nation. I have taken the liberty to list below the basic tenants of the Constitution—which every Rwandan now enjoys.

Chapter II of the Constitution

Fundamental principles include (but are not limited to):

    Equitable power sharing
    Separation of Powers
    Rule of Law
    Promotion of social welfare and social justice
    Pluralistic democratic system
    Gender equality
    Fighting against genocide ideology

Eradication of division
Promotion of national unity
Quest for solution through dialog and national consensus

Chapter III of the Constitution

Fundamental human rights include:

Every person is sacred and inviolable
All Rwandans remain free and equal
All have the right to life, mental and physical integrity
All are persons and equal before the law
Each person's liberty is guaranteed by the state
Every Rwandan has the right to his or her country
We all have freedom of thought, religion and opinion
Everyone has a right to education, private property, and land

Chapter Four: Empowering the Nation

Under the former regime, control was at the top. Economic, educational, land, and financial gains were disproportionately placed under the control of a few. Self-interest reigned, thus creating a huge divide between the rich and the poor. This regime also fostered gender and ethnic inequality.

Under the current united Government, measures are in place to combat those issues. Though we realize that no country in the world will ever be able to set up a perfect Utopia, we have worked hard to eradicate the issues that poisoned our nation.

Economic and financial gains have been addressed through the reform. Here is a classic example of what is being done: *communities now have long-term objectives to increase trade within the country, the region, the continent, and beyond.* Again, it all starts at the grassroots level.

Communities use their skills in farming. This leads to employment opportunities as people begin to work the fields. It provides income for the necessities of life, and enables parents to send their children to school. When the harvest exceeds what is needed for a community, it's traded out—into the region and elsewhere. The Government is heavily investing in communities, so that they will have what are needed to develop a productive agrarian society. With each sector of the country engaging in this type of activity, economic growth and financial gain occur for everyone.

Also, for the first time in our history, gender inequality has been legally overturned. Our country now embraces female leadership, and has provided in the Constitution that at least 30% of Government positions must be held by women. Today, we have exceeded those numbers. Rwanda is the first country in the world with 56% women in our Parliament, more than 30% in the Cabinet, and over 70% in the judicial system. Indigenous people, youth, and the disabled are all well-represented in our Parliament.

The atrocities of the past have taught us that women and vulnerable groups need to be featured in our leadership. The new Rwanda wants unfairness to be part of old history. Women from all walks of life openly participate in the process of dialog and resolution—on the community level. Many of these highly committed citizens are not paid for their services. They realize the seriousness of community involvement and their role in reconstructing the nation. They use the rights granted to them by the Constitution, and actively work to resolve community issues.

Rwandan women have also made into their primary agendas the issues of gender-based violence, maternal health, child mortality, and corruption. They are fiercely determined to see that reconstruction takes place, with justice as the foundation. Women realize that corruption in the past has brought shame into their families, and from a woman's viewpoint, corruption can abort the progress of women's advancement to their God-given potential. With due diligence, women are successfully weeding out and exposing corruption.

Women have played a most powerful, vital role in shaping laws during the reformation. During the transitional Government, women established the Forum for Rwandan Women

Parliamentarians, with their objectives being to: revise the discriminatory clauses in existing laws; push for gender equality in new laws; introduce legislation on punishment of gender-based violence crimes; and introduce that laws originate in Parliament rather than in the executive branch.

The prior system was that the Ministry of Justice introduced all the laws, but women changed that—most laws now originate from Parliament, where women have more influence to include gender perspective in every step of legislative drafting.

In 1999, female lawmakers and civil society pushed for equal inheritance and property rights between males and females, and equal inheritance between husband and wives. This is as opposed to in-laws obtaining an inheritance, leaving a young girl and her mother with nowhere to turn to. This potent legislation made it possible for women of all ages to have full rights to an inheritance, and to own land.

Female lawmakers also removed discriminative laws that restricted women from being able to represent the country in diplomatic positions without their husbands' permission, and other laws that kept women in financial servitude through not being allowed to have their own bank accounts without having a male signatory.

Woman's leadership helped to achieve a gender-sensitive Constitution, which now enables women to be guaranteed at least 30% of the seats in Parliament, under Article 9. Women are represented from the grassroots level, provincial level, and in all three branches of Government. This makes it easy to campaign or bring more women into decision-making roles.

In 2001, women Parliamentarians helped pass the law: Relating to Rights and Protection of the Child against Violence. This law criminalizes child rape. Marriage under the age of 21 is also considered rape. Women also played an active role on Gacaca Law, by adding a provision that protected sexual violence survivors. This was an extremely needed measure that allows women to be respected and legally protected while testifying against sexual violence.

However, the most significant law under female leadership was the drafting and adoption of the Gender-Based Violence Laws. Being part of the first team that kicked off the drafting process of gender-based violence legislation in 2005 was a humbling experience for me—it was finally passed in 2008. Women in Rwandan society and vulnerable individuals are fully protected under the provisions of this law. Its passage is exemplary as to why women should be kept in key leadership roles.

Women from all walks of life, including myself, made it possible for these laws to be enacted by their commitment to a better Rwanda. As a historical reference, the women listed several paragraphs below have been wonderful catalysts for change, and I should mention that most of these women continue today with the hard work of building a better Rwanda.

This is by no means an exhaustive list. The pages of history will never be able to contain all of the vital women who took part in restoring our nation. These are the women whom I walked and worked with closely. They are an integral part of my personal journey, and my story of our new Rwanda. Every woman that has ever had a part in the reformation is to be applauded, whether or not she is mentioned in this book.

These women and many others did not demand to be in decision-making positions. Instead, they made decisions in their communities and districts, working closely with other women during the transitional Government in 1994. Party and political differences were put aside. In unity, they raised their voices to put away the pains of genocide, bring healing to the nation, and empower Rwandan women's advancement.

America's former President Kennedy once said, "Ask not what your country can do for you; ask what you can do for your country." I believe that citizens providing service for the good of their country is the ultimate act of patriotism. I think it would be hypocritical of me to receive benefits when so many people are contributing to the advancement of Rwanda, and to not be an active part of the process. I am proud to say that I took an assistive role in the reconstruction process. All citizens who have participated should be proud of the good that has come out of a hugely traumatic situation.

I was young, educated, and energetic back then, and decided to use my well-honed skills to bring women's rights, human rights, and justice into the forefront. My advocacy and determination were that our new laws would be gender-sensitive, fair, and uncorrupted. I and many other activists also decided that the best way for us to do this was to stay outside of political circles—so that our work would be uncompromised by the political environment.

I was, and still am today, a highly vocal activist. I have devoted my life to helping in every way that I could, especially by getting involved in matters concerning justice and women's rights. I have worked with other women to advance the gender and leadership issues in rural communities. There were so many people in rural society that needed to learn how to organize, speak up, and empower themselves.

It was an honor for me to volunteer my services and work tirelessly without pay as a consultant. Widows and orphans were very special to me. I was a young widow taking care of many bereft orphans, and could deeply feel their pain.

Because of my intense activism on gender issues, I was a great resource for the media, which helped me become more popular. I traveled around the country, training women and Government officials on gender equality. I had access to many influential people, and used this access to further the cause of gender equality. It was important that men in leadership learned to be sensitive in that area—and my role was to help them understand exactly what gender equality means. Today, it is evident that the laws in Rwanda are sensitized because our men did listen. Not just to me, but to all of us that took part in gender education and activism.

My core values on justice, equality, and good governance are well known and highly valued. I have spoken on these values at international women's conferences and consultations, had the privilege of working with the ruling party, been involved with all levels of Government (the Cabinet, Judiciary, and Parliament), and at the same time I have been honored to work closely with the grassroots community.

I have also contributed to my country by being an active spokesperson and unpaid ambassador of the new Rwanda. I have been advancing the cause in the women's movement, and still play an active role in empowering women in leadership positions. I served as the second Vice President of Profemme after the Beijing conference in 1995; Rwandan women believed that we no longer needed to wait to learn how to lead before taking leadership. We believe in the cause of taking action toward a just course.

I have mentored women in all walks of life, in and outside Rwanda—grooming them to be fierce, capable, and confident leaders. Today, I work as an international legal and development practitioner in various transitional governments that need help with gender and development issues, as in legal and judicial reforms.

My list of the noteworthy modern women of Rwanda:

Many intelligent, graceful and valiant women have fought for the good of Rwanda. We pay tribute to those who are sadly deceased, and gloriously thank them for their noble efforts that have caused Rwanda to shine.

Ms. Veneranda Nzambazamaria:

A mentor and pioneer of activism after the genocide, this gracious woman was my mentor, and she influenced me to be the person I am today. Veneranda mentored women around the world; she is one of our heroes in Rwanda, and remains an inspirational figure at the United Nations. She boldly spoke against the abandonment of the international community during the genocide. Her untiring efforts ensured that rape was recognized by the International Tribunal, and considered a weapon of war. This heinous act was placed in Category One—War Crimes and Crimes against Humanity.

Due to her activism, women traumatized by rape gained the strength to testify, resulting in the perpetrators being brought to justice. She died in a plane crash in 2000, coming from a woman's conference in the Ivory Coast. Veneranda Nzambazamaria showed the people of Rwanda the powerful impact an ordinary citizen can have on society. The effects of her outstanding works are still shaping Rwanda today.

The Hon. Judith Kanakuze:

She headed the Duterimbere Association, a micro-finance institution that established the first Women's Savings and Credit Cooperative (Copedu Duterimbere) in the country. This bank was started as a result of micro financing, and is still one of the women's leading banks in Rwanda today. Judith helped thousands of people with financial interactions throughout the country.

She was actively involved in the Constitution Commission, pressing for gender sensitivity to be a part of the legislation. Our tremendous joint efforts on the Gender-Based Violence Laws were finalized and passed. She and I also worked together on many strategies to counsel civil society and politicians on gender-related issues.

From 2003 until 2009, Judith was an invaluable Member of Parliament (MP). Her final legacy and bold commitment to our nation was her leadership of the Forum for Rwandan Women Parliamentarians. She died in 2009, when she was known to carry her work to the hospital during her final days.

The nation has lost a woman of great wisdom and knowledge, and an outspoken advocate of women's economic and political empowerment. I personally lost a best friend, and miss her very much. We are all indebted to Hon. Judith Kanakuze for her life-changing works.

Ms. Jeanne Kadalika:

Jeanne was an impeccably brave journalist, and instrumental in exposing how Tutsi women were negatively displayed in the media during the genocide. Her invaluable work on media manipulation set a standard on how consciously we view commercials and other forms of media that portray women as sexual objects. Jeanne's active role in putting this issue in the forefront of politics and educating activists and the public is greatly missed.

Ms. Raika Felicite Umutanguha:

Raika was a committed activist, who left our country a strong and lasting legacy for the cause of liberating women. Her passion to insure that women of today and future generations would have gender equality was tireless. Being a genocide widow and survivor, she knew first-hand the trauma associated with it, and was extremely active in restoring others' lives. Prior to the genocide, she worked with the UN, and afterwards she was an outspoken critic of its failure to assist Rwanda in our greatest time of need. She also became head of Sonarwa, one of the largest and most prestigious insurance companies in Rwanda.

Ms. Kamaliza:

As a singer and songwriter, Kamaliza's guitar and voice were more powerful than any weapon used against us in the genocide. Her powerful songs brought consolation to millions—widows, orphans, victims, soldiers during the liberation, and those needing a balm for the soul. Famously remembered for her last album, *Humura Rwanda*, she is one of the most celebrated artists in Rwandan history, being my best friend and partner in the struggle. Rwanda has lost one of the most electrifying and patriotic women the country has ever known.

Kamaliza's compassion began as she watched the struggles of her people in Burundi, where she lived as a Rwandan refugee. Just trying to survive the daily battles related to issues of race, ethnicity, gender, and finding her own identity gave her much inspiration to write her songs. In the midst of all of the suffering she saw and experienced, her songs only expressed love, forgiveness, compassion, and patriotism. Those who were impacted by her music could identify with the power of her message, and embraced her as a legend.

She was constantly reaching out, encouraging the RPF that was fighting to liberate our country. Kamaliza was welcomed by the staff of hospitals and families with injured persons during the struggle for liberation. War and genocide widows and orphans across the country gained strength from her consolation. She was always unselfishly giving.

Writing this reminds me of a time when Kamaliza and I were helping with feeding baby orphans at a church in the eastern part of the country. Everyone was distraught—there were so many needs. But when Kamaliza began to play and soothe us with her songs, she brought calmness to the children, and a smile to everyone's face.

We all recognized at that moment that she was one of the best gifts to children suffering after the genocide. She continued her powerful role as "music of hope ambassador" until 1997; her life was suddenly taken away in a car accident. She is deeply loved and missed.

Having honored the dead, now I will pay tribute to those who played a critical role in the origins of the new Rwanda, and who are still advancing the vitality of our cause.

The Hon. Aloisea Inyumba:

Minister Inyumba is currently serving as a returning Minster of Gender and Family Affairs and has held other positions, including Senator and Mayor of the Eastern Province. She began her political career over 22 years ago, when she was a refugee and a university student in Uganda, and is a highly regarded political figure from the RPF.

From the time that she started working with the RPF, she kept a focus on gender sensitivity in the forefront. It is believed that it's due to her commitment and those of her female colleagues who also served in the struggle that the RPF is sensitive to the women's movement and supports the need for women to be in leadership positions.

She served along with other women Army generals during the struggle to end the genocide. She is well-known for one of her greatest contributions: exposing and ending corruption. She has partnered with me in many campaigns, as we both in our own professions seek to advance the cause of gender issues. Her humility and firm commitment to leadership and women's issues had caused her to become one of the most respected women in Rwanda.

The Hon. Speaker Rose Mukantabana:

Rose is the first female Speaker of Parliament in Rwandan history. This is a great achievement for our country—especially since she began from civil society and worked hard to move up the political ladder. She has been an active member and consultant in the local and international NGOs (non-governmental organizations) and various forums, and provided free legal aid to women throughout the country while she served as the head of the Women's Lawyers Association (Haguruka). She has also been extremely influential in formalizing laws relating to rights to land, inheritance, child custody, gender issues, and sexual violence.

Rose had a tremendous impact on my life as we worked together after the genocide, traveling to the countryside promoting gender justice. Her valuable work will ensure the rights of citizens for generations.

The Hon. Constance Mukayuhi Rwaka:

Also an MP and former civil society activist, Constance is a woman of deep Christian faith—and is highly active in the ruling party of the RPF. Her constant prayers kept us encouraged and energized for the tremendous tasks we all dealt with every day to restore our nation. She also served as Vice President of Profemme. This organization's tremendous impact on Rwanda is immeasurable. We learned how to speak out, and advance actions for peace.

She also served as a senior official in the Ministry of Foreign Affairs prior to becoming an MP. Constance was a bridge of reconciliation between Hutu and Tutsi women. She made all of us believe that we could get through the crisis together, and we did. Her long-term friendship has been invaluable. In 2003 she became an MP, where she still serves proudly with courage and commitment today.

The Hon. Connie Bwiza Sekamana:

A long-term serving MP, Connie started her political career as a young cadet from the ruling party of the RPF. She rallied hard against injustice to women during and after the genocide, making sure these tough issues went before Parliament. She has served there as a lawmaker for the last fifteen years, having held that position longer than any other female activist.

My journey with Connie began seventeen years ago as we dedicated ourselves to the cause, ensuring that adequate measures of law and justice were written and adopted into Rwandan law after the genocide. Connie is a devoted Christian, committed lawmaker, and an icon in Rwandan society.

Amb. Solina Nyirahabimana:

A former Minister in the President's office before she was appointed as the Ambassador to Geneva, Solina is one of the best strategists and legal minds I have ever known. During her time with civil society, we worked together on legal matters and finding ways to mobilize men and women in society. Our efforts have been successful. As a result, we see a very bright future for Rwandan citizens.

She has also steadily moved up the political ranks, starting as the Executive Director of the Women Lawyers Association. She has also served in the Ministry of Foreign Affairs and as Cabinet Minister in the President's Office from 2003–2011. She was recently appointed as the Rwandan Ambassador to Geneva. .

Ms. Marie-Claire Mukasine:

Marie-Claire served as the head of the Association of Women Lawyers after the genocide. She played a critical role in legal jurisprudence, and helped us to develop the implicit wording needed to create the strongest laws for the protection of women and gender justice issues in general. She has held many top positions, including ones in the Ministry of Gender and Family Promotion. She also headed Sonarwa, one of the biggest insurance companies in the country. Currently, she is serving as a highly respected senior Government official.

Ms. Godereva Mukasarasi:

A rural activist and determined peacemaker, Godereva embraced and infused the spirit of unity throughout rural areas, making it possible for Hutu and Tutsi women to come together and rebuild their lives and communities. Under Godereva, women literally "fixed" their problems by repairing their homes, standing on their rooftops to work on them. She challenged women to step beyond their pain, and into restoration.

Her work has astounded our nation. She has received national and international recognitions in her advocacy to promote peace and harmonious living among all women in rural areas. Presently, Godereva is pushing for human rights for the so-called "unwanted children" born from rape during the genocide. Her tireless efforts have empowered women throughout our nation.

Ms. Zainabu Kayitesi:

The head of the National Human Rights Commission, Zainabu is a passionate leader and influential woman in Rwandan society. After the genocide, communities suffered with lack of trust issues. Her humility and sincerity helped people to believe and have confidence toward the legal system again. As a result, she was able to be a "bridge" between the community and leadership. She rallied for justice and women's rights in the Government, and is now the head of the National Human Rights Commission—continuing to support women's equality before the law.

Ms. Immaculée Habiyambere:

Immaculée was a young female activist after the genocide. Her exuberance in youth is a shining example that age should not be a factor when deciding to become proactive. She has ably helped several women's organizations, such as assisting with Profemme's campaign about issues facing women, and also in tirelessly advancing the cause of the Campaign for Peace.

Some of the major issues she has dealt with include women and peace initiatives, justice, reconciliation, conflict resolution, and HIV/AIDS. Immaculée also played a critical role in helping politicians understand the needs of grassroots communities. As a national consultant, she is still actively involved today.

We partnered together and provided training sessions across the country about the Constitution and gender training. We are still in contact today, and are always in consultation about issues on good governance, justice, and women's empowerment. She is still actively involved, especially in reaching out to rural women—and empowering them with her consulting skills.

Ms. Immaculée Mukankubito:

Ms. Immaculée was another young social activist involved in the movement that had a tremendous impact on shaping our new Rwanda. We were known as "the biggest mouths" in the NGO community, particularly in one of the largest rural networking groups, Reseau des Femmes. We were always trailblazing the country—speaking boldly on anything that benefited peace, reconciliation, and the women's movement.

Our friendly association is still close today. She trained hundreds of women, and campaigned immensely for inheritance rights. She is still actively involved at present and reaches out to establish development in other regions, such as the DRC (Democratic Republic of the Congo) and Burundi.

Ms. Suzanne Ruboneka:

Mama Susan—she is our Sage! No one will ever forget the wisdom and mentorship of Susan Ruboneka. She used her insight to mentor lots of women, many of which are in Parliament today. It has been an honor to know her, and she remains the face of our long-term Campaign Action for Peace initiative we started in 1996. Susan used her expertise to help communities understand health issues, women's issues, family issues and gender equality. Susan also did an outstanding job instructing women on family planning. She has always been an active member of the NGO community, and actively works with Profemme.

Ms. Esther Mujawayo:

She is one of the founders of Avega-Agahozo, an association of genocide widows. Rape was an unspeakably barbaric crime against women during the genocide. Women across the country struggled with telling their story publicly, so that justice could be done to the perpetrators. Esther gave them a voice, helping women become strong enough to testify and end victimization—in order to empower them to move forward.

Avega became a highly powerful collective. The group brought the issue of rape as a genocide crime to the International Criminal Tribunal for Rwanda. Avega was also instrumental in supporting survivors and those victimized by rape during that time. The group continues to be a critical part of the new Rwanda, actively promoting women's causes and encouraging women to take leadership positions. Esther currently lives in Europe but still plays an active role in gender issues and conflict resolution, and she continues to speak out against war and genocide.

Ms. Jeanne d'Arc Kanakuze:

"Get up, and get what is yours!" This is Jeanne's powerful motto; it compelled women in both urban and rural communities into action. As a civil society activist, her free spirit and ability to speak the language of the people has made her one of the most popular advocates of our time.

She is personally an inspiration to me, because she has the uncanny ability to find joy in the most adverse times. That a joyful life can be fun again is her attitude—it is infectious! She is a role model for single women, showing that you can raise a successful and educated family. Later in life, she returned to school and got a Bachelor of Arts in Education, and then a Master's in Gender Studies. Jeanne d'Arc is a remarkable woman.

Ms. Ingabire Marie-Immaculée:

When Marie-Immaculée speaks, Rwandans and those in the region listen. She is one of the most dynamic, informed, and powerful media voices and civil society activists in the country today. She boldly speaks out and stirs up activist causes about corruption, women's rights, and the right to life for those in Rwanda and other struggling countries—such as the DRC and Burundi.

Her background in journalism and work as a paralegal make her an invaluable resource to law enforcement and the promotion of anti-violence laws for women and children. She is currently the chairperson of the board of Transparency Rwanda, a watchdog institution that fights corruption in the country and also in the region. She is an inspiration and mentor to women and upcoming journalists. It has been an honor to be one of her associates.

As you can clearly see from these many shining examples, our Rwandan women truly value their powerful influence in shaping policies that affect the entire country. At the same time, they are advancing feminism, allowing our nation to see the wisdom, insight, and value of women. The women are doing such an outstanding job that Rwandan society can soon envision a day when all of our brothers, fathers, husbands, sons, and grandsons will no longer speak or hear any word of discrimination against their female counterparts. *Everyone will grow up feeling equal!*

Women throughout Rwanda have long been hard-working activists for positive change. They have insured true safety for women and children from acts of violence. They have opened the doors for women to take leadership roles in a country once dominated by male political influence that often diminished the role of women. The new Rwanda takes the best ideas, skills, and leadership from all of its citizens—female or male. It is an enlightenment that is making Rwanda into a highly progressive nation.

The stability of a nation also revolves around the health of its citizens. Healthy people keep the economy thriving. Rwanda has invested heavily in healthcare, making it mandatory. Almost 90% of Rwandan's have healthcare. The cost to the public is minimal in terms of the benefits it brings to the nation. Since the reformation, the monies that have been collected for healthcare have gone into providing coverage for our citizens, improving the salaries of medical staff, and into purchasing state of the art equipment. People are professionally treated—and are being treated well.

Prior to the reformation, it was not unusual to see people fall down sick in the halls of health centers and hospitals, and serious lack of attendance to the suffering. Medical staffs were severely overworked and underpaid. But since employers now contribute to the system, there is enough financing to improve care and exponentially raise the level of technology; even the worst cases of disease that people fear, such as malaria, are being successfully managed or eliminated.

In Rwanda, healthcare is treated as a human right, and the Ministry of Health makes sure that each individual is covered and understands the benefits of our system. As a result of this aggressive approach that our Government has taken, we are now experiencing reduced death rates, an ever-increasing life expectancy, and are increasing the degree to which people are able to enjoy their daily lives.

We want the rest of the world to know about the good that has been accomplished, and hopefully our system will become a model for those nations wishing to develop a progressive healthcare system. We also hope that countries debating the value of healthcare for all of their citizens will also consider our model in their debates.

The next massive change for our nation was to tear down the educational system that heavily favored the rich and privileged, and to open the doors to educational equality. This has been an extreme undertaking, and we still have a lot of work to do. But the good news is tremendous change.

For example, during the former regime, we only had one university—under the control of those seeking their own self-interests. Under our present leadership, we have over 18 universities, colleges, and technical schools, both Government and privately owned.

This has paved a way of accessing education through various means. The Government selects high-performing students and provides them with scholarships to attend public universities. Meanwhile, those who are able to obtain self-funding can easily enjoy education through private universities and colleges.

There have been, however, some observations that the poorest of our nation are not able to attain their higher educations, such as at the university level. The communities and Government are constantly working on ways to improve this situation. The universities and schools developed in the last seventeen years in Rwanda include, but are not limited, to the following:

1. Kigali Institute of Science and Technology (KIST), Science and Technology
2. Kigali Institute of Health (KHI), Medicine and Nursing
3. Institute Superieur d'Agriculture et d'Elevage (ISAE), Agriculture
4. Umutara Polytechnic University (UP), Technical Training in various vocations and Vocational Training
5. School of Finance and Banking (SFB), Finance and Business
6. Kigali Institute of Education (KIE), Education
7. Institute for Legal Practice and Development (ILPD), Judicial Training
8. Kicukiro College of Technology
9. Tumba College of Technology
10. Kavumu College of Education
11. Rukara College of Education
12. Kibungo School of Nursing and Midwifery
13. Byumba School of Nursing and Midwifery
14. Kabgayi Nursing College

In addition to our public universities, the Government has put policies in place that allow business and investors to open private universities, colleges, and vocational training to help emerging needs from the working class, which may want to learn other skills or obtain their education in the evening hours. So far, more than seven such institutions have emerged, and more are still opening. Here are some of our private universities and colleges:

1. Institut d'Enseignement Supérieur de Ruhengeri (INES), Arts
2. Institut d'Agriculture de Technologie et d'Education de Kibungo (INATEK), Arts and Sciences
3. Université Catholique de Kabgayi (UCK), General Arts
4. Université Libre de Kigali (ULK), Liberal Arts
5. Université Laïque Adventiste de Kigali (UNILAK), General Arts
6. Rwanda Tourism University College (RTUC), Management and Tourism
7. Faculty Theologie de Butare (FTPB), Theology

As a result of these increased educational opportunities, more and more of our people are taking full advantage of them. This has enabled them to get better paying jobs or even to start their own companies—as their literacy and affluence are greatly increased.

Women have also gained significant independence, and are better equipped nowadays to contribute to the financial needs of their families. Statistics show that the rate at which female salaries exceed male salaries is increasing. More and better education has also had a positive influence on child bearing, because people are now planning their families based on how much time they need to set aside for education.

Another good trend has been that people who had lost the opportunity to acquire education in the former regimes are returning back to school to get advanced degrees. The big boost in salaries gives people the confidence to purchase homes, because they feel they will have the financial ability to pay a mortgage. The laws have changed so that a husband needs the wife's signature before taking out a mortgage. This way, both their incomes are included in figuring out the house payments.

Likewise, our young people are taking advantage of their educational opportunities—while the country is doing all that it can to ensure job availability to meet the influx of students exiting the institutions. It's attempting to meet the demand with job sources within the country, the region, and beyond—and encouraging self-employment.

Quality education is normally guaranteed when better early childhood education is implemented. Our country is practicing some of these measures on the pre-school and primary level, providing nine years of basic education and making sure that all preschoolers have milk and nutritional food; this was introduced by President Kagame. It lifts a huge burden on struggling families. I know of no other country where those in authority go door-to-door making sure that children from the ages of three to six are in school, taking advantage of this nutritional opportunity.

Another important initiative provided under the guidance of President Kagame was the implementation of laptop computers in the hands of all students. The prior regime only wanted a hoe in the hand of every child, thus enslaving them to a laborer's status. Kagame, being the visionary that he is, wanted more for the children. He wanted them to have independence and economic opportunities—therefore, the decree was a laptop for every child.

So far, that goal has been implemented in 60% of the targeted primary schools across the country; 100,000 laptops have been deployed in the capital and provincial schools since 2008. This collaboration is between Rwanda, friends of Rwanda from the United States, and wealthier school districts supporting rural areas. The Government is responsible for funding this project, without taking contributions from other groups. And the Ministry of Education is responsible for distributing and administrating this noteworthy project.

The One Laptop per Child program aims to improve the educational conditions of teachers, children, communities, and schools in general. There is a team of Rwandan experts and international consultants in the country who travel to communities, teaching children and teachers how to use their new laptops.

It is overwhelming to see how this wonderful project has brought excitement and advanced learning in the lives of children, teachers, and parents! The hope of the nation is that one day our economy will be strong enough to support top quality education for all, and to afford all Rwandan children with a better education—so that they can compete on a global level.

The pride in having an educational system that is accessible without discrimination cannot be taken for granted. I never imagined my country would ever have opportunities for educating its citizens like this. *It sends shivers up my spine!* People nowadays realize the widespread power of a good education. It is an equalizer between the rich and the poor. It provides the means for people to reinvent themselves. This new Rwandan system has brought such pride to all of our families.

There was a time when a wife and husband stayed home at night, or spent a lot of time watching sports on TV (for those who could afford it). Now, one or both of them goes to school in the evening, while the other one helps the children with their homework, in many cases by using the Internet. Families are attending evening classes like never before. It is a main priority. The Government is so supportive that many businesses, including Government offices, are closed by 3:00 P.M. in order to give people time to go back to school in the evenings.

Because of education, people are now developing an entrepreneurship mentality. The very business of starting a private university is an example of this. Some types of businesses that have proliferated as a result of advanced educational opportunities are: law firms, IT businesses, tourism, expansion of the food industry, grocery store chains, the food packaging industry, hotels, the entertainment industry, the printing industry, and even the fashion industry (on a small scale).

Business is growing every day, and some are able to export. That is a tremendously good sign for the economy! As Rwandans look to the future of their educational advances, they know they have opened the door for its citizens to compete globally, giving them the power to live anywhere in the world—with an education equal to any country's standards.

Chapter Five: Healing the Nation

With the legal and governance structures now in place, the Rwandan people have a safe place for true healing to begin. Though reconciliation was the toughest hurdle to overcome, we faced the world with a true desire to bury our past, just as we buried our dead. Our mission was twofold: to forgive and reconcile with ourselves for killing each other, and to forgive and reconcile with the international community that abandoned us in our hour of abject terror. No family was left unscarred or without loss.

We knew that communications would play a vital role in our reconciliation, but getting on the road to where people would openly discuss the terrible events that had traumatized them was difficult. Despite it all, people courageously began to take part—all across the nation. The dialog began, and a clear and motivated resolution followed.

We would gather in various places, sitting in buildings to have meetings that had no agenda, no direction. We only knew that it was important to meet and have the faith to believe that something good would happen. Sometimes, the only thing we could do was cry. Other times, our strength rose beyond our pain, and we discussed the horrific crimes, the violent rapes, where to bury our dead, and the urgency to find a place to live.

We talked about who would care for the orphans, and how to get urgent medical and emotional help for those raped brutally. We had to work through how any woman would be able to relate to any man again without paralyzing fear. Those talks had to be done, as traumatic as they were. We certainly had to help our men as well. They saw their wives abused and killed before them. Out of those ashes came our improving the Ministry of Gender and Family Promotion, the focus of which was to work closely with other ministries and civil society to strengthen policies and help vulnerable groups particularly in rural areas.

Then there was the issue of the Hutus. They were not all involved in the bloodshed, yet every family had lost something—for example, their dignity—and from this they bore the feeling of being ashamed to be a part of the ethnicity that had brought about the slaughter. Some were married to Tutsis, and now family relationships that were severed would have to be restored. Everyone in the nation had been impacted. Reconciliation was for all. We had to become unified. There was no other option.

One of the most gut-wrenching points of discussion was how to deal with the criminals and their acts of violence, especially those who murdered innocent children in the name of hate against Tutsis. I, being a part of the legal system, have heard the confessions of criminals, and listened to them describe their deplorable acts of murder against innocent children.

It was truly revolting. People lived in the same community with their remembered assailants. That is chaotic, maddening to even think about. But we had to get past our anger and pain and deal with the situation. No one will ever know what so many individuals have gone through on a daily basis, but Rwandans overcame for the good of the nation, together restoring our solid value and complete pride.

As we continued to dialog on topics too numerous to mention, we came up with the structures that would help rebuild our society. We created a system to ensure that our future generations will never re-experience the past horrors. Our new role as Rwandans is to keep telling our story. It must remain in the history books. It must be told throughout the world, so that people of other nations can avoid the tragedies that we suffered. We must never be silent about this matter, and we must be vigilant against it. We must always let our generations know the cause of our genocide.

It was a master plan of disseminated hatred and division that was financed by taxpayers of both the international community and the developed world. France and Belgium fueled and financed the atrocities. We must let them know that the international world did not intervene, because Rwanda was of no economic interest to them. When they turned their backs on us, that made the insurgents feel invincible and escalated their violence.

Whether the world ever admits to their part in the demise of our nation, it is already fact. Our country has chosen to forgive, but those facts should never, ever, be erased from our history.

Chapter Six: Reconciling the Nation

The aftermath of genocide left the nation in ruin, burdened with many complex issues to resolve. There was militia violence still taking place in the northern part of the country, and the Government was struggling to bring innocent civilians back from violent refugee camps in the DRC. Through that attempt, agents of militias disguised themselves and came back with civilians, starting to fuel the killings again.

In an effort to fight the militia, the Rwandan Army deepened the operation along their borders and in nearby refugee camps in the DRC, which led to more militias disappearing deep inside various parts of the Congo. This was not only a challenge to the Rwandan Army, but also to civilians, who were being taken by the militias to be used as human shields and slaves.

The overwhelming challenge was how to safely bring back innocent civilians without risking the lives of those they were trying to save. As a result, military and political conflicts escalated between Rwanda and the DRC. Civilians who weren't yet repatriated from the DRC were caught in the crossfire, facing violence as the fight between the Rwandan Army, the militias, and the other factions was waged in the jungles of the DRC.

Meanwhile, our country was suddenly inundated with the uncoordinated support of the international community, despite the fact that they'd abandoned our country in the time of its greatest need. This caused massive political problems. During this time, there were others in the international community who offered assistance—but were later identified with having allegiances to the enemy. Their actions seemed to assist the former regime militias to regain control.

Unfortunately, dealing with the chaos became very political; Rwandans had to take control of the confusion caused by the international community's "support," and actually aid in Rwanda's destiny. In addition, people were so busy rebuilding that they didn't have time to grieve. In this highly toxic environment, Rwandans knew they had to reign in problematic areas as quickly and effectively as possible. The nation stood up boldly, determined not to be dictated to by the international community or be hindered by the continued assaults of the militia.

Rwandans now successfully began to manage the country and swiftly bring resolution through homegrown solutions unique to us. Some groups which handle our continuing needs include: the National Unity and Reconciliation Commission, the Gacaca Court System, the community work done by genocide criminals commonly known as travel d'interest generale (TIG), as well as Umuganda, Ubudehe, Itorero, and Imihigo. All these initiatives were the foundations of healing, forgiveness, confession, and reintegration in Rwanda.

The speed of the Gacaca justice system made it possible for the perpetrators' crimes to be addressed and for fair judgments to be rendered. It also allowed the victims and the perpetrators to meet face-to-face, while our leadership worked hard to expose the truth, bring accountability, and put an end to impunity. It helped the citizens of Rwanda to bring closure to their tragic situations.

The law defined the different categories of crimes. Category One crimes included those who planned or directed the genocide. These crimes were judged by either the ordinary courts or by the International Criminal Tribunal for Rwanda (ICTR), established by the United Nations to respond to the 1994 acts of genocide. Category Two included those who committed crimes with the intention to kill, or whose actions led to death. Category Three, as defined by the law, related to those who committed crimes leading to serious assaults. Category Four was for offences against property.

All but the Category One crimes were tried by Gacaca judges in the communities where the crimes were committed, or where the victims suffered violations by the hands of their killers. This power for communities to solve their own problems was an excellent path to bring accountability and foster healing.

The TIG community is not only given a chance to serve half of their sentences outside prison doing community work, but it also reinforces unity and national reconciliation process, contributing to the economic development of the country. The TIG program focuses on the goals that Rwandans need the most: fighting impunity, promoting unity, reconciliation, and contributing to national development.

Most of the prisoners have reformed, and are aware that the destruction they inflicted on humanity was unnecessary and should never happen again. It has proven successful to allow the convicts to interact with those they harmed through community development. It not only helps both parties, but most convicts find it is easier to confess their involvement in the genocide and ask for forgiveness when it allows the victims to feel confidence and trust for their Government—allowing themselves to truly forgive.

TIG's community services are partly used as the criminals' sentences or part of their sentences. From the Government's perspective, it would be illogical to keep all prisoners behind bars when the entire Government and its free people are working excruciatingly hard to rebuild the country that these prisoners destroyed. Similarly, the Government feels that it is unjust for thousands of prisoners to be funded with taxpayer money in order to sit in jail on a life sentence. They should be busy paying back their debt with hard work, while the taxpayers' money is better spent on healthcare, education, general infrastructure, and other aspects critical to rebuilding our bright new nation.

The TIG community has participated in various activities, such as road construction, rebuilding homes for genocide survivors and other people without shelter, building schools, farming, and other developmental undertakings. TIG allows those guilty of crimes to have a chance to rehabilitate what they have destroyed while, at the same time, reconnecting with their communities. It is a way for them to come face-to-face with the destruction they have brought, to reintegrate, and to see both where the country has come from and how good governance is now allowing all citizens to participate equally.

Many of the TIG community whom I've met are very grateful to this program, because they know that the severity of their crimes may well have kept them in jail for life or have them executed. For the Government and communities to allow them to take part in the nation's development is much more than they have expected. TIG allows their sentences to be expedited, so that they can rejoin their families—which they never thought they would see again. The TIG program has definitely provided an excellent way for their debts to society to be repaid.

Rwandans believe that rebuilding communities paves a way to reestablish life again, and to advance development. TIG reinforces that fact of unity and national reconciliation and contributes to the economic development of the country. It enables the incarcerated to acquire new professional skills that help them facilitate their reintegration into society. All convicts are trained in human rights and other related fields of Government doctrines. The culmination of these efforts builds lasting peace in the nation.

Only Rwandans who know these matters understand that reconciliation is a long, tedious process, requiring much strength and adequate time and interaction between the offenders and the offended. The involvement of prisoners in community work before they are totally set free gives the involved parties a chance to slowly reconcile. This is when they sit down and ponder the futility of continuing hatred and having an unnecessary dichotomy between them. And in the economic point of view, TIG has put hundreds of thousands of people into active work.

As people in the TIG community have labored to rebuild the country, so have the other citizens. One of the most phenomenal aspects of Rwandan society is Umuganda, a public community service that predates colonial times. It is a systematic approach for persons 18 years and older to voluntarily contribute their time, labor, professionalism, and workmanship to the country. This participation extends from the average citizen to the leaders of our nation, and to the local police and the military. The spirit of every citizen taking ownership of the land and contributing to the wellbeing of their neighbors makes Rwanda one of the cleanest and most unified countries in the world.

Umuganda takes place during the last Saturday in every month between 7:00 A.M. and 12:00 noon. Only critical services are exempted, such as hospitals and personnel on call. During this time, people provide services to their community such as cleaning the streets, cutting grass along public roadways, and landscaping the community.

The public is also engaged in building and renovation projects that include construction of homes, schools, hospitals, etc. Even members of the military join in these building efforts. Others provide free professional services for members in the community; this includes free medical services, free classes offered by educators, and free dental services.

Umuganda provides a platform to build community involvement, once again focusing on dialog and resolution. The head of the community, called the Chief de Mudugudu, is responsible for selecting topics of discussion for the month. These discussions cover critical issues relating to the country's wellbeing, such as land development, combating domestic violence, prevention of HIV/AIDS, security within the community, health issues, business development, and youth employment.

Since these communal efforts include persons from all walks of life, it is an excellent time for the average citizen to be able to speak with their leaders and authorities. It has also been a time to invite persons from other localities to dialog and reconcile with Rwanda. Ambassadors from countries such as the United States have actively participated in these endeavors. All these activities boost economic development, further the cause of reconciliation, advance unity, and make the country less dependent on foreign aid.

Ubudehe is yet another reconciliation mechanism that focuses on the eradication of poverty, especially in rural areas. Ubudehe embraces the spirit of unity and wellbeing, as members of the community come together to tackle economic development issues. Historically, this system was applied to help the indigent and persons unable to work. Community members would help with the planting and harvesting for those less fortunate. As a result, members of the community investing in each other's wellbeing all celebrated a successful harvest. Community members were proud to lend assistance.

In reconstruction, Ubudehe operates on a much larger scale. It not only encompasses agrarian assistance, but all measures of business development and financing. It promotes the idea of learning new skills to eradicate poverty, bringing the rural community into dialog with the local and national Government so that action plans can be developed. It also encourages the local community to stay proactive and advance their own causes on the grassroots level to bring economic growth. Compassion and peaceful coexistence are among the many benefits that Ubudehe had brought to Rwanda.

Imihigo Initiative – Delivering the Promise

This outstanding initiative was brought to try and encourage accountability and sustainability throughout the country. Like any other historical and ancient practice that dates back in Rwandan history, Imihigo was used to make sure that people delivered what they promised to the public. It provides a mechanism for ensuring better accountability and service delivery by increasing understanding of roles and responsibilities of both leaders and citizens.

Imihigo focuses on obtaining timely results, and everyone works their best to ensure this happens. Imihigo in the new Rwanda works as a wakeup call. It combines the understanding of responsibilities given to local leaders with matched resources being provided to obtain objectives. Through Imihigo, local authorities have learned planning, budgeting, monitoring and implementation of their goals.

Imihigo is always evaluated by community members. Furthermore, Imihigo has allowed for rapid increases in meeting several key sectors in education, health and services, poverty reduction, and MDGs (Millennium Development Goals)—the achievement indicators. Officials at all levels are specifically thinking about Imihigo with a focus on results, and ordinary citizens are given a greater role in policy formulation and evaluation.

Itorero – the Youth Camp

This extraordinary initiative was established as a way to teach Rwandan values to the young generations. Itorero was used by our ancestors to teach the children love of the country and our people. The young would be taught patriotism, love of the nation, wisdom, and the values of living a dignified lifestyle regardless of circumstances.

Through the reformation of the nation and the reconciliation process, Itorero was taught as a way to bring about understanding among the youth. In its camps, young people share personal and social experiences of life, relationships, sports, and engaging in dance. Rwandan culture has incomparable values—and we have to protect them. In addition to having fun through the program and our beloved traditional dances, our youngsters do a lot of mingling. Itorero teaches them about national unity, social solidarity, patriotism, integrity, bravery, tolerance, the dos and don'ts of society, etc.

The young generations are also taught the history of Rwanda and how "divide and rule" from the colonial powers made matters worse until divisionism led to genocide. As a road map for the new Rwanda, participants of Itorero take advantage of learning Government policies—such as Vision 2020 and EDPRS (Economic Development and Poverty Reduction Strategy)— which guide all reforms and initiatives in the country.

The unique Rwandan practices of the Gacaca Court System, TIG, Umuganda, Ubudehe, Imihigo, and Itorero have all brought healing, restoration, and new development to the country on all fronts. We are well aware now of our many and varied successes. We want the image that the world sees of Rwanda not to be represented by our past tragedies, but rather by our exemplary actions that have built a productive and thriving nation with pride.

Chapter Seven: Reconciling with the International Community

Rwandans have demonstrated to the world the power of national reconciliation. We are extremely proud of how we united, taking a bleak part of our history and rendering it powerless to keep us enslaved to pain and bitterness. What we have accomplished so far is one of the best acts of redemption in the 21st century.

However, the circumstance of genocide in our country was not only Hutu against Tutsi. The international community played a huge role in supporting a militia regime, fueling the atrocities and abandoning the country at its ultimate worst time. What the international community did is tantamount to treason. They dishonored covenants, agreements, and peacekeeping mechanisms that were supposed to be enforced during times such as genocide. Their actions gave strength to the militia murderers to continue their killing spree, empowering them to make them believe they were invincible. We can never forget this.

However, the Rwandan way is one of forgiveness, being a caring and nurturing people. We are an understanding people. As a nation, we decided to learn from the international community; we purposed to forgive them and to start another chapter, where we would be the masters of our own destiny. We would welcome their support, but only on our terms. We were now battle-hardened, and knew that in times of turbulence we would have to depend completely on ourselves and never, ever be open to dependence on another nation for anything, especially our security. We survived and became stronger, wiser, and more determined than ever to create a new Rwanda based on national planning and execution of those plans by Rwandan measures.

In the new Rwanda, the international community must be in partnership with us. They are no longer able to impose their agenda on our nation through excessive financial inputs. We are no longer willing to be merely on the receiving end of those financial "gifts". We learned from past regimes that unless there is good governance and a planned and organized use of international money, those funds will be used in corrupt ways, or in many cases the funds will be used to kill citizens. Those funds would benefit only those in power, and the nationals would not benefit.

Directly after the genocide, the international community waltzed into our country handing out so much money it was unbelievable, with a "business as usual" mentality. We put a stop to it. In a collective voice (from the grassroots to those in leadership), we spoke up and demanded equal partnership. Our terms stated: if you really want to be a part of reviving our nation, then you need to hear the voice of the people. You need to find out what we need, instead of telling us what you will do for us.

No international support in the new Rwanda was going to have strings attached or be unaccounted for by the citizens, nor solely directed by an outside country. I would say that the genocide empowered us—a blessing in disguise, indeed. We were at that time and still are today an unstoppable nation, whether we have the support of the international community or not. Why? It is because we rebuilt our nation, while many other nations abandoned us.

I don't wish to imply that we don't appreciate the help that the international community has provided in the aftermath. I am only pointing out that when you abandon a nation, you cannot return to it in the same position you had prior to leaving it. Most of the international community had good intentions, performing good deeds to help our country after our great devastation, but the implementation was poor. You have to rebuild trust and be willing to negotiate on new terms, and this was often not well done.

We also had to make it known to parts of the international community that did not have good intentions but were rather motivated by self-interest that their deplorable actions would no longer be tolerated. We made it clear that if you intend to use funds and assets in any inappropriate measures, you can take your resources back to your own country. Or you can give your resources to a country that doesn't have a plan and is willing to be the recipients of your tainted "goodwill".

But Rwandans have a plan. You are welcome to be part of it, based on the agenda set forth by our people. Our voice was made clear, heard all the way to the United Nations level. Little by little, the international community has begun to accept the new Rwandan way, and we have developed good partnerships with them.

One thing we did appreciate from the international community was when they sent their leaders to our country to publicly apologize and get a better understanding on what had happened, and why their abandonment cost our nation so much grief. It was not on their part to sit from a distance and say "we are sorry," but also to actually come to the nation and become a part of our struggle. While we will never fully be able to understand why they did not abide by the treaties, their sincere presence made a profound difference and was a part of our national healing.

I particularly remember former US President Bill Clinton. He regretted his prior actions and said, "I am sorry, deeply sorry." Then he put his words in force by starting the Bill Clinton Foundation in Rwanda. This foundation set up clinics to help support those women who were raped and infected with HIV/AIDS.

Our nation has worked with this foundation to make sure that it takes care of the needs of the community in ways that are best for Rwandans—not the interests of the Clinton Foundation. By President Clinton personally visiting our nation, it showed how important this partnership had to be.

The Secretary-General of the United Nations at that time was Kofi Annan. He was another person that left his "ivory palace" to experience the devastation first-hand. He apologized, and our nation accepted it. He also realized that Rwanda was not going to allow the wealth of the United Nations to be merely thrown at them. The United Nations would have to abide by the needs of the Rwandan people. In my opinion, the respect that we gained from standing our ground is what makes the relationship between the UN office in Rwanda and Rwandan citizens one of the strongest ones in Africa, if not in the world.

What we did to restore the relationships between our country and the international community was a remarkable feat. It was done with unity, wisdom, and diplomacy. It showed the world the power of forgiveness. It also proved that partnerships were possible.

As a country we made our needs known. We understand what we have and where we are, and we continue to welcome the international community to work with us—within those means. This is what we have: a small country whose precious resources and citizens must be protected; a history that burned the reality of genocide into our very souls, and how it must forever be fought; and the ability to look into the future and not the past.

Finally, we have a message for the world: Rwanda provides hope for the nations. Countries rebuilding their governments and demanding democracy can learn from us, avoiding what happened to us. As the international community understands what we have, they can help us develop. *We want them all to listen to us—and they have, for the most part!*

Our leaders know the voice of the people, because they are elected from the grassroots. So when the international community comes in to help, we want them to respect the voices of the grassroots. We want them to listen to all our leadership, not just in the hierarchy of the political system. Our leaders are ordinary citizens committed to protect Rwandan integrity and dignity, and our leaders are everyday parents, mothers and fathers who care for the interest of their children's education and healthcare. They come from churches, from schools, from rural communities, and so much more—the international community must always listen to their voices.

Genocide has caused us to transfer the lessons we learned from that experience to long-lasting governance. Our laws have changed, our people have been empowered, and we encourage the international community (through partnerships) not only to come and help us, but also to observe our ways. The things that have made our nation stronger could be implemented in other nations, especially the struggling ones.

It is amazing how the international community knows about the horrors of genocide, but does not know how far we have come in redeveloping our world. They have no idea of our glorious renaissance. We encourage the international community to be ambassadors for us. Struggling nations need hope. If Rwanda could emerge from our ashes, surely other struggling nations can overcome their challenges and attain a glorious future.

Each time an international community member acts as a partner in a developing country instead of an overlord, it builds trust. People that trust each other can work together, and when people work together, nations prosper. To do it any other way is to colonize people in the 21st century. Partners will listen to the needs of the people and respond. They will use their money, resources, knowledge, and expertise to respond to our needs. This attitude and these actions are so much different from the past!

Before, the international community would be the one to set the agenda. For example, they would provide resources for us to develop our agriculture. If we didn't use it on agriculture, they would remove their resources and leave our country. This type of pompous agenda was no good, because we were already skilled in agriculture. What we needed were decent hospitals, and clean, potable drinking water.

Nowadays, all these things have changed, while we set the agenda. If we need hospitals or clean water and they are willing to support this area of development, then we welcome them. This is the right way for the international community to become involved in nation building—and it is the only way it will be done in Rwanda. Our history has taught us that anything less is corruption and colonialism. We have established laws and security factors to deter any revival of the old ways.

There will always be those in the international community that will never be a part of this unusually good development. France and Belgium have never admitted their involvement in Rwanda's atrocities. They have given refuge to those who slaughtered us. Canada, the USA, and other Western countries still provide safe haven to the militia from the 1994 genocide. Some of these countries knowingly chose to violate conditions established by the genocide conventions.

Nevertheless, Rwandans have again chosen to walk in forgiveness. We partner with these countries in other aspects, but we don't shy away from reminding them of their wrongdoings. They chose to abuse their taxpayers' money to feed and nurture individuals who committed atrocities in another country. Our way is simple—we will not allow pain to hinder our progress. This mentality has earned us respect from outsiders, and through that we have attracted trusted partners.

Rwandans are resilient and forgiving people. This is exactly what we want the world to know.

For the last seventeen years, we have been glad to say that we have great partners. Our landscape is filled with new homes, renovated hospitals and emerging clinics, new schools and new businesses—all because many people in the international community listened and supported our agenda. This has gone a long way toward rebuilding our sacred trust.

Chapter Eight: Reconciling with Self

The process of reconciliation and forgiveness in Rwanda was different from the normal way that people forgive those who have wronged them, in that the damage was so massive that people had to put their own personal hurts on a secondary level. Without doing this, it would've been impossible to move forward. We were decimated, destroyed, and lawless. We did not have time to consider ourselves. Immediately, we had to bury our dead, build our homes, find a place for orphans, and restore our legal and governance systems.

It was only when we got the foundations established that we could deal with our own sorrow. When the pain came crashing down, many of us regretted being born as Tutsis—while many Hutus who hadn't been involved in the massacre were ashamed of the hurt their people had caused. As a nation of people we were perplexed, faulting ourselves and asking this burning question: *What could have we done differently?*

We wrestled with how people with the same language, the same traditions, and living side-by-side, regardless of historical political or colonial context, could allow themselves to be divided to the point of destruction. And yet, we had to forgive ourselves. There could be no more division. Tutsi had to forgive Hutu, and Hutu had to forgive Tutsi. We could not hate ourselves, or whom we were born to be. Some of us would need forgiveness. Others would ask to be forgiven. We knew we had to move on, but the means of personal forgiveness was no easy matter.

People began to develop their own ways of coping, and working through the act of forgiveness. Some sought help from churches; others got assistance from friends and family; and still others needed help from institutions. No matter the pathway, Rwandans became active in healing themselves. They knew the value of first forgiving self, then the community, and afterwards the Government.

It was important for Rwandans to believe that being born a Tutsi was not a sin. This freed the Tutsi people to understand that bad things happen to all people. It was also important for the Hutu to believe that being born a Hutu was not a sin, and that all Hutus were not murderers. These were very complex issues. Slowly, we came to see each other as being first and foremost fellow Rwandans—one nation, with one undivided pain, and with the same future dreams of peace, freedom, and happiness. This helped us to have compassion for one another and begin to heal.

Layer by layer, we began to deal with the deeper issues. How do you forgive the people that have murdered your family? Can you truly forgive those who have killed your loved ones, without dishonoring the dead? How do you forgive the father of your child born out of rape? How do you forgive the men that gang raped you and gave you HIV/AIDS? How do you help the orphans understand what happened to their parents, and teach them to forgive? How do you reconcile with your Hutu neighbor who is in so much pain for what other Hutus did? These, among many others, were very intense, delicate matters.

I believe that people finally realized that unless they forgave, they would be enslaved to pain and bitterness. They realized that staying in that type of bondage would be a living death. It was not worth it. So, we forgave. You can forgive without forgetting. We can never forget what happened, because remembering is what will help those acts never to be repeated. Yet, we can emotionally release those who hurt us, for our own good.

Forgiveness is an act to be practiced by everyone, each day. We all hurt in different ways. We can be criticized, ignored, misjudged, and misunderstood. No one is exempt from hurting, or from tough times. The true meaning of forgiveness is the same all over the world: renounce anger, stop being angry, and pardon those who have caused you harm. This is what truly helps the emotions to settle, and allows you to move on.

When Nelson Mandela was elected President in South Africa, he could've used it as a platform of revenge. But he called out to his people to forgive one another. After 28 years of being tortured and abused in prison, his immediate act was to heal the nation through forgiveness. He realized that forgiveness was a powerful idea. We Rwandans came to learn as well the power of that action, which is potentially quite dynamic.

But it takes a lot of time to heal. People that have been abused and traumatized cannot just begin to "let things go." Damaged relationships need time to sort things out, letting God bring them to a place of forgiveness in good time. Yet with goodwill, a stout heart, and the determination to forgive, victims can be free and offenders can be pardoned. The biggest reason to forgive is because it releases us from the bondage of negativity. Otherwise, we will carry around pain from other's actions, and only punish ourselves.

Real forgiveness is about self-healing; it is so powerful that it can reach out to people who are far away, decades from us, and even the dead. Forgiveness has the power to break all hurtful ties and associations, get rid of all offenses, and offer us a new spiritual and emotional start. Rwandan people have suffered together, healed together, and must continue to rebuild our nation and our lives—through forgiveness—together.

Section Two:

Laying the Right Foundations

Chapter Nine: Integrity, Trust and Freedom

The decline of Rwanda actually began with the fall of the monarchy, and it continued through the colonial era. This caused many basic foundations of trust and integrity in our country to be eroded completely. Therefore, to see Rwandans nowadays working together to build up trust and integrity within our nation is an incredible act.

We are grateful for the work that the united Government has done, and we often hear people praising them for good works; but our ordinary citizens cannot be left out. They have played a tremendous role in bringing us our renewed unity, trust, and integrity. Our citizens began to see the need to support the Government, and the Government began to see the need to support our citizens. The people and the Government understood that since their problems began with mistrust, learning to trust would bring about numerous much-needed short- and long-term solutions.

In order to begin this process of trust, the Government realized it would have to abandon the old ways. This meant it had to make sure that it was working for the people's interests, and not its own self-interests. In the past, the Government seemed to trust everyone but its own citizens. It was because they put the interests of the colonial powers before the needs of the people that so many atrocities had happened. In the new Rwanda, the Government would have to trust its people, and especially learn to trust the judgment of its citizens. They would have to listen to each and every community across the country, and attend to its needs.

As a result, our new governance would begin from the grassroots community and spread up, straight to Parliament. It would no longer work in reverse, where the rules and regulations started with Parliament and then passed down to the people. The citizens of Rwanda took control of their Government officials, making them accountable to their needs and interests. Thus, the Government was to be directed by the voice of the people.

This was a greatly complex task, because now the country had to develop internal structures that would make it possible for the people's voices to be heard. They also had to come up with policies and procedures for the voice of the Government to be heard by its citizens. In essence, the citizens and the Government opened a unique communications system— whereby there would be constant dialog between the citizens and the leadership.

Everyone would be informed, and everyone would have a chance to provide input. I have traveled around the world, and have not seen a system of governance as extensive and effective as the one created by our Rwanda.

This system is open to all. The youth have become inspired and heavily involved in the system. Those who were victimized have the opportunity to have their matters duly heard, and justice is served. The ordinary citizens now have an accessible place to express their deepest aspirations and the wildest dreams they have for their country. The Government has a place to present their plans, and to work with the citizens to develop those plans for the good of the nation.

This level of transparency has brought not only trust, but also an overwhelming level of patriotism. All of this helps to make Rwanda a highly progressive nation. It enables us to nationally resolve problems, such as the eradication of poverty, the development of a highly competitive educational system, and the development of a healthcare system that benefits all citizens—all while setting long-term goals for future generations.

Citizens are taught about our system of governance. That way, they know where to start the process if a grievance must be addressed or when a new innovation needs to be witnessed. It starts in the community level (Umudugudu) and then expands to wider neighborhoods, through structures called cells. The cell representative reports all related needs to the sector. The sector representative reports these needs to the district. The district representative reports the needs to the province. The province representative then finally reports the needs to the Cabinet, and eventually to Parliament.

This chain of communications makes the voice of the people heard, loud and clear. When the people's voices reach Parliament, they expect it to legislate what they said. They are not seeking Parliament's or the leadership's approval. In the new system, the Government is the people. The leadership is only in place to carry out the needs of our people.

However, people in leadership can voice their concerns in the same manner as everyone else. They live in our neighborhoods, too. If they have a need, it goes through the same system of deliberation. But their position of power no longer allows them to circumvent the system. Their position is one of stewardship, not of dictatorship.

Engaging within this system of communications has built trust. The citizens and the Government are listening to each other—they've become one.

Chapter Ten: People Power

To me, there is nothing more fascinating than watching the citizens of Rwanda take part in the governance of their country. It is truly "people power," starting with the grassroots community—a dynamic interaction between the young, the old, men, women, and persons of all educational and economic positions. No one is excluded from these dialogs. In my experienced observation, the youth and the women's movements are literally exploding!

The young are bold, fearless, and not wanting to be tied down to the ways of the past, or impacted in the future by the horrors of war and genocide. Therefore, they are extremely active—making Rwanda the place they want to live in and raise their future generations. Our women are strong, determined, and wise. They are extremely active, because they don't want to see the atrocities against women and children ever occur again. They value their political system as the means to ensure their safety.

Women are working hard throughout the country, in both paid and *pro-bono* positions. They have decided that money will not determine their level of input. Their objective is to restore the nation, without allowing money to influence their decision to take part in the restoration process. Many of the women in today's positions of power and influence started out in *pro-bono* positions, well over a decade ago. They learned the system of governance by moving up through the ranks. Now they are in positions of great authority, in paid positions. They learned to be sensitive to the needs of the community because they were a part of it, and they worked very hard to get in leadership positions so that they could do even more for their country.

As a result, our women have been involved with economic development, economic growth, business, small enterprises, and micro-financing. These efforts have tremendously impacted communities in the area of advancing national wealth, educational opportunities, healthcare opportunities, building healthcare facilities so that women can give birth safely in hospitals, and bringing more awareness and solutions to HIV/AIDS, malnutrition and poverty issues. Women are extremely sensitive to these problems, and they are doing their part to improve the condition of women and young girls. It's an extraordinary work.

Men have also played an active role during the reformation. However, the focus in this section is not on our men, because it is not uncommon for men to take leadership positions. What I would like to note herein about our men is the role they're taking in family planning. This is unusual in Rwanda. However, in the genocide's aftermath, men began to really take note of the issues that women were dealing with. They began to listen to the community dialogs, which often discussed population issues.

As a result of women's voices ringing throughout the country, these men began to see the need to be more sensitive and supportive of their wives' health issues when they were solely responsible for family planning. They became more aware of the health risks associated with taking the pill, or injections for birth control. Men also began to learn more about HIV/AIDS, working to find solutions. In addition, our men became more sensitized to gender issues, gender equality, and the support of female leadership.

As a culmination of this, the men in Rwanda (in general) have become deeply supportive. They are listening and allowing their influence to make Rwanda better for women and young girls, and are more than ever taking an active role in family planning—even if it means getting a vasectomy. Men are also actively and positively responding to the act and discussion of protected sex, as a response to family planning as well as HIV/AIDS prevention.

These measures are improving relationships between men and women, between male leaders and female leaders, between husbands and wives, and assisting in how men relate to their offspring. As horrible as the genocide was, as an unforeseen result, the landscape of gender relations in our nation has significantly improved, and the establishment of trust has increased.

As a whole, our citizens realized that people should've sounded the alarm to prevent genocide. They also realized that somebody should have screamed louder during the genocide, before things still continue getting worse. Silence was the public's worst enemy, one they inflicted upon themselves. Now the country is charged up—*people power!* Our people are strict sentinels, actively ensuring that the political environment which allowed for the planning of the massacres is forever banished. At the forefront of this banishment are the women, because we were often the objects of the most horrific acts.

Chapter Eleven: Understanding Governance

In the old regimes, wrongful laws were forced upon our citizens, with mindsets of hatred and mass manipulation. Again, the public would not break its silence—or at least speak up to any degree of effectiveness. This corrupt form of governance led to the disintegration of Rwanda. Those ways have been abolished, hopefully never to return.

The Government does not force its laws upon our people. If our citizens do not agree to certain types of laws, there are legal actions that can be taken where they are not even enforced. This is a powerful form of democracy, one that the most democratized nations do not enjoy. In the modern Rwanda, the Government can put forth new policies, while explaining them to the people through the channels of communications that have been established from the grassroots and on up. It relates these policies in simple laymen's terms, so that all can understand them.

The people deliberate all such policies from one community to another. Massive dialog occurs—advocacy, question and answer interchange, solicitation for more detailed explanations, etc. Dialog continues until the people reach a consensus on the benefits or detriments of a policy. If it is found to be in the best interests of the people, then they inform the leadership to implement the policy. But if it is not found to be in the people's best interests, then they will inform the leadership that the policy cannot be enforced.

The system of trust established after the genocide is what enables our people to rely on the Government to enforce their wishes. The Government knows that if they ever betray their trust, it will immediately bring the nation to arms. It is openly known that the people of Rwanda will never be silent about anything important, ever again. Over the years, the Government has done a wonderful job. They like the trusting relationship that has been established between our leadership and our citizens. Whenever they are introducing a policy, they take it through the process slowly and deliberately. As people truly feel they understand, then the Government successfully implements changes for the good of the nation.

Due to this sound leadership, Rwanda is developing rapidly, and people are eager to find out what is happening within this relatively small country that is nonetheless exploding into the global scene. Rwanda can no longer be defined by its past of genocide. It has become a powerhouse of growth, rapidly becoming the most advanced economic hub on the entire African continent. The news media and the World Bank have praised our nation as being a highly developing and economically growing country.

Today, our Rwanda shines. It is clean. It is peaceful. It is loved and admired by the people and their Government. The Government is the people, the people are the Government, and they both continue to build a legacy of trust and integrity, thus becoming a better country. There is a national pride that glows from all of its citizens, including those of Rwandan birth who live abroad (the Rwandan Diaspora). We also keep the pulse of what is going on in the home country, actively asking how we can play a role in our country's positive transformation.

We are so proud that we are united again—one language, one tradition, one dance, one dream, and one united set of cultural practices—and once again honoring the traditional values and pride of our ancestors.

Chapter Twelve: Understanding the Spirit of the People

Rwandan people are *doers,* not mere dreamers! We created our new image by doing. This is part of our culture. In most countries, people write about what they want to become, and then work toward that objective. In our culture, we act first and then write about it later!

In a lot of cultures, people spend a lot of time talking about what has happened, trying to explain the situation and constantly writing about it. We are different. We spend time rebuilding—and not trying to explain what happened. We know what had happened. We trusted in a corrupt government, and it failed us. We have addressed that corruption and have established a new trust in the "Government of Unity." We have moved on!

To the cultures that like to write on our history, we encourage them to write about the new Rwanda, instead of focusing and dwelling on our past in order to push their own political agendas. You need to change with us, friends; that is what would most benefit the world. For the last seventeen years, we have been busy rebuilding the country, witnessing the benefit of that approach, and we want the world to write about it.

We want the media to have the right message. This message is that the people of Rwanda are completely proud of their actions to create a better destiny. We now work willingly for the good of the nation. Our Government does not have to compel us to work. We work because it is in our culture to be doers, and this brings about patriotism.

The Government has done an outstanding job creating our vision. The people understand this, and are moving forward with it. The Government has also done a wonderful job showing us that if we act in unity, using our own skills and resources, we don't have to be dependent on foreign aid. This teaches us to live within our means. That, in turn, reduces our dependency on outside support.

For example, at this time we don't have a lot of materials and goods that we can export. But we do have land we can develop—right in our own backyards. If we care for and develop that land, we can leave it to our children; it will provide them with economic stability. Each parcel of land that we own becomes sustainable, and we won't have to look to another country for food, or to teach us how to develop our land.

We have even developed a master plan for our capital city and the other major cities around our country. Having a Rwandan plan motivates us to work hard until we achieve it. It also helps us attract interested partners to interwork their own designs into our overall plans. However, hidden agendas are no longer welcome within our country. Only transparent, worthy partnerships will be welcomed.

I may never live to see the entire Kigali master plan be completed. Even so, the fact that we have planned well into the future generations makes us unique on the African continent. The people know what the Kigali of the future looks like, and we work actively to build it, even though we know only our future generations will be the real benefactors.

When visitors come to Rwanda, they are highly impressed by our work ethic and the development that they see. I am so proud to be a part of it, and truly hope that we can be an inspiration to struggling countries. The leadership of this world can learn a lot from what we have done and are doing. If our nation could be turned around, there is hope for any nation that truly wishes to rebuild, and for any Government willing to cease feeding their self-interests for the good of the entire people.

Unfortunately, for all the good that we have done, we are not without dissenters. We have had people question if the nation is truly reconciled. We have had people accuse our Government of manipulation, and say that we are actually a dictatorship regime. Others have attacked the nation because they are jealous of our restoration. Also, there are still countries that have become havens for those who participated in the atrocities.

But for whatever reasons that people speak negatively about us, attempt to impede our progress, or work against us by harboring criminals, the spirit of our nation is destined to be victorious. We experience a new victory every day, with every new building, every young child that gets a decent education, and every woman empowering herself to leadership after being victimized. For each day that the sun rises, we honor our dead and restore our pride by building a legacy of peace.

This has not been an easy journey. We lost over a million people in 100 days. We live in the same neighborhoods with the perpetrators. Try to grasp this difficult situation: victims living right next door to the ones who abused them. Try to understand having to ask your neighbor to forgive you when you have their beloved relative's blood on your hands. Yet, we have done it. We have overcome.

We deserve the credit for this hard road to forgiveness, reconciliation, and restoration. It is shameful that our dissenters have attempted and still attempt to discredit and impede our progress. It is shameful that some of our dissenters would prefer that our country had been wiped out. But like a phoenix rising from the ashes, we strive forward, and we succeed. I truly believe that the love and dedication our citizens have for Rwanda will overpower anything negative said or attempted against them.

Rwandans also have a great weapon to use against dissenters. It is the same weapon that brought us the reformation—*our voice*. We always need to inform the outer world, and to report about our good news. This is counterpoint to the worldwide media, as they are experts on bad news. They get their funding to promote only the most horrific stories, and hardly anything to report the good in the world. A friend of mine who works for primetime media has confirmed how difficult it is for reporters to get funding for the good that ordinary people do.

But we must continue to step forward, to gain positive recognition. We need to actively look for those who will report good news. Surely there is some unified media voice that will speak the truth, go beyond the drama, go beyond the bloodshed, and report positive things that are going on in the world. If not, we need to create our own media—and speak our own truth—because surely we have a much greater story to tell.

It is not enough that our recent history ended with genocide. To be honest, even when the genocide was reported on, it was not done well. In my opinion, people never got the whole story. Every media outlet was providing fragments of the truth. CNN had one story, CNBC another, and on international television, the BBC had yet another one. For the most part, mainstream media reporting is dependent on funding; corporations have corrupted the media, due to their self-interests. Such self-promotion stifles the truth from being well-communicated.

The wise men and women of the world need to use common sense and bring truth to the airwaves—and not allow commercial and self-interests to prevail. In Rwanda's case during the genocide, there were numerous other entities (not connected with the main media outlets) which were presenting their own versions of that story. Perhaps if these people had really known how bad it was, there would have been more of a global cry for help. There has got to be a way to set that story straight, and show the realistic advancements of our time.

It amazes me that even when I do public speaking at universities or other places where I travel, many people do not know where Rwanda is, and they only vaguely recall the stories about our genocide. That is still another indicator of poor media coverage. Yet when I get past the bad news and begin to tell them that we are the first country with 56% of women in Parliament, they are hugely interested in knowing more about us.

It's hard to conceive how people have learned about the 1994 genocide, yet do not know where our country is—not having any updates on Rwanda in seventeen years. All they know is about the past! They have no idea of the wonderful things going on right now. We Rwandans need to become ambassadors, in order to proclaim the good news of Rwanda. We need to challenge people, especially those interested in the 'global village' concept, to build peace through communities, and begin fighting for the release of good news. Rwandan ideas may be utilized by other nations with the same energy, drive, and spirit. We must change the world before the world changes us.

Ordinary people in Rwanda have revolutionized the nation. It has taken a lot of hard work. It has shown those in the world that were watching our resilience—beyond all measure. But there are still more people to tell. By becoming personal ambassadors, we can let the world know that our efforts really made a difference. *In fact, the whole purpose of this book is to give ordinary Rwandan people and others their long overdue credit for an extraordinary piece of work.* If we were given credit for the wrong that was done, we deserve to have credit for the good we have done.

I would like to see more Rwandans do what is right for the country—to be the change you want to see in others. That is the position I've chosen, to write about the good happening in the country, speak out more, engage more, and volunteer in/visit other communities and countries. That is what I do. And what I learn from other nations I bring back to Rwanda, to keep on rebuilding.

But above all, we must inform other nations how we did it! Tell them what is happening in Rwanda now in loud and joyful voices; make friends with other countries, using the social media for all it's worth. The Internet is a powerful outlet to inform the world of your viewpoints and perspective without the control of media politics.

Go for it—invite people to come to Rwanda! I'm always inviting people to visit Rwanda. Not because they bring humanitarian support, or invest money. I want them to bring their thinking, their insights, their viewpoints, and as much time as they can spend in our country. As they get inspired and involved, then they will become ambassadors for us.

With our voices, we can reach out to people who have no way of knowing how to move on. We will reach out to women in the world who have no way of knowing how to move up the political ladders and make changes for the good of their country. We can reach out to men in other developing nations, and teach them the value of family planning. We can reach out to young people, and encourage them to make their nation a place to live forever, instead of running away from their country. People have the power to make incredible change. People have the power to make their countries shining stars.

Gandhi said, "Be the change you want to see in the world." That can start right in your own country. Make it the best, and then be the best citizens. There's no need to have a "brain drain" on your country, where the nation's best and brightest leave. Yes, visit other nations and learn from them, but stay connected to your home country. Bring back your knowledge, and make your home country the best place in the world. If you must work in another country, live there—but still give some back.

Visit often. Make your voice known. Let the people of the country know you are a proud Rwandan, wherever life may lead you. Tell the world you are proud of your nation, and invite them to visit. I once asked my children to pick a country where they would take their dream vacation. I told them I was totally willing to pay for it. You know what they told me? They wanted to go home to Rwanda! This made me a beaming, proud mother. Indeed, they visit their motherland as often as they can, even if it is short due to their busy school schedules.

There was once a time when we were all ashamed to be Rwandans, but that time is no more. So Rwandans, shine for your country. Speak up for Rwanda. We have made our nation one of the best in the world; now go out and talk about our love, our hopes, and our aspirations that will give struggling countries hope—and how we have worked as one with our Government. We truly are a shining light for all to see!

Chapter Thirteen: Advancing National Priorities and Compliance with the International Agenda

In the past, the international community directed the actions and plans for our eradication of poverty—as they do in many other nations. But now, we no longer wait, and have taken it upon ourselves to set the agendas. Our main agenda can be found in the Vision 2020 and EDPRS policies that guide all our reforms and initiatives. These plans were in place before the UN established their MDGs. We are glad that we took a proactive stand, and have developed plans that are also a key part of the global agenda.

Some of the issues included in our plans and the global plan are: eradication of poverty, elimination of discrimination, protecting the environment, advancing educational reform, and promoting quality healthcare. For Rwanda, these elements must be put in place without pressure from the international community. Understanding those priorities made it easier for our districts to start planning clearly. It meant that all communities, whether rural or urban, needed to speed up the initiatives that fed into our national Vision 2020 and our poverty reduction strategies.

Once the plans were in place, then our country began to market itself as the best partner for multilateral and bilateral institutions. The World Bank, the IMF, the African Development Bank, and many others are now enjoying partnership with a country that has its own home-grown plan that can be realized by ordinary people. These entities were mainly interested in partnering with us because they saw we had a plan that is unusually well made—for most developing countries.

Although insufficiency is still an issue for our country, we are making such strides against it that you see the landscape of poverty being erased, albeit little by little. Even with the small amount of resources we have, plus the fact that we are a land-locked country, nothing has diminished our ability to move forward. Daily, we see improvements. Rwandans know we will see our goal of poverty being eliminated come to pass, because we have a roadmap. It's no longer a matter of whether it will be accomplished; it is only a matter of when!

UN Secretary-General Ban Ki-Moon praised Rwanda just a few years ago for accomplishing the MDGs, especially the achievement of Goal Three—promoting gender equality and empowering women. He said, "Women now comprise 43% of elected local Government leaders, and hold more than half the seats in Parliament. With this, Rwanda offers an outstanding example, not only to other African countries, but to the entire world."

In education, Rwanda has already achieved gender parity in primary school enrollment. In healthcare, there was a 30% drop in the maternal mortality rate between 2000 and 2005. In economic security, legal reforms have been passed to enable both men and women to inherit land. The Secretary-General also highlighted the importance of political diversity, and encouraged the Government to work for broad-based participation of all political parties, civil society, and media organizations in the legislative election process.

Rwanda has been on the international agenda of educating the world as to how the nation has been able to accomplish so much within the last seventeen years. There is no doubt in my mind that we will be able to reach the Vision 2020 goals in the shortest amount of time, and will also accomplish all of the MDGs before 2015. To date, we have achieved about 75% of the goals identified.

Other Aspects of Gender Equality

The following list shows our accomplishments in gender equality:

1. The Constitution guarantees gender equality. It has been mandated that women fill 30% of all decision-making roles. In validation of this mandate in 2008, 52% of Parliamentarians were women, and 32% of Ministers and State Ministers were women.
2. Inheritance laws were enacted that provided liberalities and successions of land tenure, to give men and women equal rights.
3. The National Women's Council was established, to ensure that the mandates for women are actively enforced.
4. The media has spread gender awareness, gender training, and gender sensitivity messages across the country.
5. Rwanda has achieved gender parity in primary school enrollment, and the rate of enrollment is very high. It has increased from 76% to 90% within the last few years.
6. Gender sensitivity is now being used as a strategy to reduce poverty.

7. Rwanda has ratified policies of the CEDAW (Committee on the Elimination of Discrimination against Women), the Beijing Platform, and other international instruments into the Constitution, legal documents, and various national policies.
8. The CEDAW and the Beijing Platform have been translated into Kinyarwanda.
9. Women are inheriting land, due to newly modified family and land laws.
10. Female poverty issues are being addressed and supported by the leadership, and provisions have been made to guarantee funds to poor citizens—particularly women.
11. Women and men are playing equal roles in the community mediation justice mechanisms. Women are a major part of gaining broader unity and reconciliation, and they have played significant roles, such as serving as Gacaca judges.

With as much work that has been done in the area of gender relations, the country must continue to push for more improvement, especially in the area of education. There are still female students lagging behind in educational achievement and access—especially at the secondary and tertiary levels. In these areas, there is often a lack of enrollment, lower rates of performance, or an inability for females to complete their educational processes. Women's rights activists continue to push for affirmative action in some areas. There has also been a significant increase for women enrolling in the sciences, engineering, and other male-dominated fields at the university level.

However, the issue we're dealing with here is not whether men are resistant to understanding the need of women's advancement; rather, it is a question of awareness. There's enough political will at the decision-making level, and enough women in the leadership to push for the right agenda. But much work is left for civil society and the private sector to make gender issues known. Nonetheless, proper actions are being taken, as gender studies are slowly being integrated into the primary, secondary, and tertiary levels. Our future generation of leaders will have a much broader understanding of gender issues in their fullest form.

Despite policies that have made great progress for women, a number of social and institutional barriers continue to prevent females from attending schools and universities—and from performing equally with their male classmates. The prioritization of science and technology within the educational and development policies of the country may act to further exclude female students, unless actions are taken to promote women's participation in these fields. Lastly, addressing gender equality in the educational system, with a focus on improving educational outcomes for females, is imperative to equitable development and women's human rights within our country.

Other Aspects of Education

There has been an outstanding effort to improve the educational system. Under the stewardship of First Lady Jeannette Kagame, the Imbuto Foundation has held ceremonies around the country for the last seven years to reward girls who have excelled in national exams—the top performers in primary grades six, senior three, and senior six.

Many of these students are given scholarships to attend prestigious schools in our capitol city of Kigali. This is encouraging, especially to the more needful children coming from poor families in rural areas.

The foundation has become a model, encouraging rural girls to excel even higher. Local Government leaders, community members, the National Army, and the police have joined residents in many districts to build classrooms with better facilities that empower girls to stay in school. The new school buildings have private areas to separate the girls from the boys, such as restrooms and change rooms. Parents, teachers, university students, and Government officials voluntarily take part in building new schools and refurbishing old buildings to meet the new higher standards.

The Government has also stepped up its efforts to help girls enrolled in the nine-year basic education program to stay in school. According to UNESCO, the current enrollment rate is 98% for girls and 97% for boys. This is the highest enrollment rate in the region.

One of the many challenges facing our schools is a high student-teacher ratio. Currently, it is 75 students for each teacher in public schools. The goal is to reduce that to 45 students per teacher. There is now a mounting need for female science teachers, while our country is constantly exploring ways to get basic teaching materials, books, computers, and lab materials. Electricity also remains a challenge, especially for schools and students in rural areas.

The goal of the Rwandan Government is to make sure that everyone has at least nine years of basic education; it must be achieved for every Rwanda child. It is believed that a basic education will increase our literacy rates. The development of advancing the nine years program began in 2011. We believe that by doing so, we will have a far more literate society 10–15 years from now. We also increased the marriage age to 21 years, so that will give our citizens more time to focus on education.

There are many benefits to having an educated society. But the primary benefit is that it will help reduce poverty, while it will also improve the way people take care of themselves health-wise, and it will increase political participation and human rights awareness.

The Government is also very active to ensure that brain drain will not happen in the country. As a result, the smartest and best minds have incentives to return to their communities, whether urban or rural. The Government and civil society have worked together to raise the issue of decent life opportunities—the lack of which is hindering the young generation in returning to their rural villages to perform required services, such as practicing medicine. This led to the Government providing incentives, such as scholarships for master's degrees and high raises for doctors who practice five or more years in the remote areas.

The Ministry of Infrastructure and the local governments also work to make sure that electricity, clean water, roads, and schools are extended to the rural areas—so that people don't feel obliged to live in the capitol city of Kigali to get all their needs met. Slowly we go, but we are steadily improving! And the Government is extremely proactive in making sure that education is a huge national priority.

Other Aspects of the Economy

The World Economic Forum reported in their annual Global Competitiveness Report that Rwanda ranked 80th globally out of 139 countries analyzed. The report assesses business efficiency, innovation, financial markets, health, educational institutions, infrastructure, and other factors affecting the economy.

The report attributes Rwanda's remarkable ranking to the progress the country has been making, commenting that Rwanda benefits from strong and well-functioning institutions with very low levels of corruption. Rwandans credit this to the Government's non-corruption policy. Our nation's economy was also highly praised for its level of innovation for this stage in the country's development. The country has grown 10% in the areas mentioned above.

The World Economic Forum also stipulated that at least one in five delegates at its 2011 high-profile conference should be female. Rwanda met that stipulation. This move was part of a wider drive by the organization to promote women's place in business globally. Even in the US, chief female executives lead only 12 of the fortune 500 companies.

International Conventions and Treaties

Rwanda has an aggressive plan to make sure that at least 50% of those who can read and write are aware of commitments that countries make to the international community, through signing conventions or other treaties. The Minister of Foreign Affairs is responsible for carrying this out. The nation has decided to only sign agreements when our leadership and our citizens have been adequately informed about their contents. In the past, the leadership signed agreements to go along with international plans without being fully aware of what was being signed, because they placed a higher value on being part of the international community than on the good of the country. In the new Rwanda, this practice has been eliminated.

Conventions that were signed seventeen years ago (after 1995) were clearly discussed, consulted upon, and understood within the leadership, which either ratified or objected to the plans. The enacting of this critical dialog has worked in the best interests of the country. The level of commitment to the wellbeing of our country from the leadership has been extraordinary. Though no Government is perfect, the zeal of Rwandan citizens and our leaders is pressing to make the country into a golden paradise.

Why not, after the tremendous grief we have so vastly suffered? Again, we have learned from our sad mistakes—and that is the greatest gift that has come as a result of our genocide.

Other Aspects of Agriculture

President Kagame continues to be prominent on the world stage, delivering the 2010 Oppenheimer Lecture at the International Institute for Strategic Studies in London. He also gave the keynote address at the 2010 30th World Food Day Ceremony, at an event held at the Food and Agriculture

Organization Headquarters in Rome, calling upon governments to eliminate the massive hunger that is still claiming lives. Rwanda continues to make good progress against this, appearing in the 11th position on the ActionAid's list of developing countries in the fight against hunger.

Since the beginning of 2011, no district is below the required food security base, and there is reason to hope that Rwanda's hunger will be completely eliminated. The Government has picked out four areas where it is placing its energies: the One Cow per Family Program, the Land and Crop Intensification Program, the Rice Program in the Marshlands, and terracing.

The number of small farms with access to quality seeds, fertilizers, and tools is increasing, and the Government is doing everything possible to equip them what they need to achieve positive results. This includes expanding irrigation and supporting environmentally sustainable production methods to tackle the endemic problems of soil erosion in the country. Investment in agriculture rose by 30% between 2007 and 2010.

Other Aspects of Land Ownership

The fair distribution of land helps every citizen to advance economically for future generations. Technology also plays a big part in that system of distribution. For example, one of the things that used to be an issue within the country was that land was never shared equally; the inheritance between men and women was never protected. The new Constitution ensures that everyone gets their share (50%), and ensures that each citizen gets a share of land, where they can feel they legitimately belong.

Rwanda is one of the smallest countries in the area, particularly in East Africa, in the Great Lakes region. Yet, it has one of the biggest practices for strengthening the economy, with land sharing being duly enforced. Everyone is given an equal share. As mentioned before, the primary purpose of land sharing is to eradicate poverty and make sure that land is a part of development. It is a human right for citizens to have land of their own.

The people depend upon the land. It is the job of the Government and the law to make sure that the people who depend on the land have ways of using and acquiring it, and to use the land appropriately. Leadership has made it a priority to ensure that the land benefits the citizens, and is not sitting idly.

Communications and Technology

Rwanda has been elected to the International Telecommunications Union Council. This is a United Nations agency that is responsible for coordinating effective development and use of telecommunications strategies globally. Moreover, the Government and communities implement its integrated socio-economic and ICT Policy and Strategies to facilitate the process of establishing a prosperous society that is globally competitive. That spirit allows all Rwandans to feel that a great future lies ahead.

As the world advances technologically, Rwanda wants to be the hub of East Africa—if not the whole continent. Rwanda already respects and appreciates the rapid changes and advances that are brought about by technology. In this respect, the Government works with people to reform ICT policies, strategies, and plans that must be part of the overall vision for the social and economic development of Rwanda.

Even if it remains a challenge due to other factors, I am always struck by the fact that everyone—the Government and the people—believes that to modernize the Rwandan economy and society we must use information and communication technologies. This is a swift solution to accelerate development and economic growth, while advancing national prosperity and global competitiveness.

Women in Leadership Initiatives

The latest statistics on women's participation in Rwanda include:

1. Parliament (lower chamber)—56%
2. Senate—35%
3. Ministers and Ministers of State (Government)—30%
4. Permanent Secretaries—50%
5. Supreme Court (judges)—42%
6. High Court of the Republic (judges)—70%
7. Gacaca (judges Inyangamugayo)—35%
8. Governors of Provinces and Kigali City—20%

In a recent report published by the Royal Commonwealth Society and Plan UK (a children's charity group), it was noted that Rwanda was ranked 10th among 54 Commonwealth Countries, just behind the UK, and ranked the second-best country in Africa to be born a girl (amongst those in the Commonwealth). The report compares how well females are doing in society as compared to males in the country, measured by eight indicators. The dates on the indicators reflect the various aspects of life, ranging from raw survival to systematic achievements.

Rwanda scored highest in political participation globally, receiving the highest marks for low fertility rates of girls between 15–19, and the highest marks for reducing the gender rate of pay gap. In terms of education, females are now staying longer in school—but this doesn't mean that staying in school longer increases literacy. The report suggested that it is political will and not economic wealth that is most important in advancing gender equality, highlighting poor countries that did relatively better than some rich countries.

Healthcare Insurance

Rwanda's universal health insurance coverage, commonly known as Mutuelles de Santé, was initiated to strengthen the quality of healthcare services and adequate access to treatment. It is highly important for the new Rwanda to not only address the common diseases in the country, but also to tackle new challenges posed by the pandemic of HIV/AIDS. Rwandans believe that quality of care must be a national priority in order for citizens to maximize their health potential. Mutuelles de Santé covers more than 90% of the nation's population, and its benefits are clearly demonstrated through increases in health indicators, specifically life expectancy.

According to a recent report, Rwandan women will live three years longer than the average male (age 59 for women, 56 for men). Rwanda allocates 18.8% of its annual budget to the health sector, and is on track to enter the pre-elimination stages for malaria. According to the malaria task force, the country has brought down the disease by 70%. Between 2001 and 2010, there was a 61% decline in deaths caused by malaria.

The ability to improve case management for victims increased from 77.4% to 85.7% from 2006 until 2010. Children under the age of five who have received treatment within 24 hours increased from 62% to 89% in 2010. Among pregnant women, such rates increased from 60% to 89.2% in 2010. The country intends to reduce malaria by 90% by 2012.

Our country has made great strides in educating our population about malaria; the people are totally committed to fighting this abysmal disease. We are proactive in getting clean water supplies, using mechanisms to decrease mosquito hatching, and using mosquito netting.

Concerning HIV/AIDS, the nation is committed to eradicating this dreadful scourge. We refuse to be identified as an HIV/AIDS-ridden nation. It is a stoppable disease that kills—like any other similar disease. We are not intimidated by this growing epidemic. We are vigilant to find a solution to the problem, and have great hope that the end of the epidemic is in clear and present sight. Rwandans are committed to achieving the MDGs and universal access to HIV/AIDS prevention, care, treatment, and support services for all of its citizens, especially our women and girls.

In support of the MDG (goals three and six)—to promote gender equality and combat HIV/AIDS—the Government has prioritized HIV/AIDS and gender issues throughout its guiding policies, including Rwanda Vision 2020, the EDPRS 2008–2012, and the National Strategic Plan for HIV/AIDS

2009–2012. Substantial progress toward achieving universal access can already be seen, particularly in our current coverage rates for PMTCT (preventing mother-to-child transmission) and ART (antiretroviral therapy).

In addition, the recent adoption of a National Gender Policy has cemented our commitment to protecting and promoting the rights of women and girls in the context of HIV/AIDS. The provision of quality services to prevent mother-to-child transmission of HIV/AIDS is essential to prevent mothers from dying and babies from becoming infected with HIV/AIDS. Through coordinated efforts, Rwandans have made substantial progress in scaling up the availability of PMTCT services, as well as integrating services and increasing women's attendance at antenatal consultation.

As a result, 68% of HIV-positive pregnant women in need of ARVs (antiretrovirals) to reduce the risk of mother-to-child transmission received them in 2009 (7,030 HIV-positive women and 10,300 estimated women in need of ART). This figure represents an increase from 56% coverage in 2008, and is a significant step toward the 2012 target of 90%, with more than two-thirds of pregnant women eligible for highly active ART (HAART) during pregnancy receiving it in 2008. In 2009, 1,160 HIV-negative women in serodiscordant couples also received ART to prevent the transmission of HIV.

Family Planning

According to the World Health Organization, vasectomy is one of the safest and most effective methods of contraception. Its advantages over female sterilization include: lower rates of postoperative complications, shorter recovery time, reduced costs, and an increased involvement of men in the reproductive decision-making. It is estimated that 700,000 Rwandan men will enroll in voluntary vasectomies and circumcisions in the next three years. In the process, they are also advised to use condoms. Reports indicate that Rwanda is the only country in Africa using non-scalpel vasectomies, which is the latest birth control method for men.

Community Health Workers

More than 80% of Rwanda's population lives in rural areas. The majority of the people have to walk for over three hours to the nearest health facility. In order to improve health conditions, the idea is to get health facilities closer to the community. One of the goals of the Millennium Development plan is the deployment of 60,000 health workers in villages all across the country. Interventions addressing the health of the community play a significant role in strengthening the broader health system.

Our health workers, on a ratio of two women to one man, are elected at the village level and are answerable to the community. The Ministry of Health has equipped them with skills to provide services for conditions like fever and malaria, HIV/AIDS counseling, and to follow up with pregnant women. Health workers focus on all levels of assistance—curative, prevention, promotional, and rehabilitative. This leads to people being diagnosed earlier, and increases the ability to prevent many diseases.

The role of the healthcare workers is not only to assist in bringing methods of healing, but also to educate the population. That role should never be diminished. They are also to actively solicit community involvement in the health and health education process. It is vital that citizens understand what health aspects will impact them the most. Increasing the level of awareness ensures that every citizen is provided enough sound information to help in making informed healthcare choices. The various communities obviously now understand that once they follow what is good for them, they are preparing for a better future—and these circumstances will benefit not only them, but also the future generations.

National Security

Rwanda has exemplary Army officers who are a real reflection of the kind of leadership our Rwandan Defense Forces (RDF) has. We specifically acknowledge the efforts of the RDF and the National Police for immeasurable security in the country. People sleep and walk peacefully, and visitors coming to Rwanda notice the calmness in the country the minute they arrive. They feel loved, welcomed, and protected.

Most Americans believe that Rwanda is safer than most of the major cities in the US. Women and girls feel safe on the street. Peace flows freely, everywhere in the country. We have lovely supermarkets and nice quality restaurants open for 24 hours—without the fear of being robbed.

Rwandan forces not only keep peace, they advance peaceful methodologies in the country. Ordinary Rwandans treasure and protect the peaceful efforts maintained by our national security forces. Rwanda's National Police and our defense forces respond faster than western countries in time of disasters, natural hazards and accidents. They are well-trained on gender violence, domestic violence issues, and child protection. When they are called about these issues, their maximum response time is 20 minutes.

These capable men and women in uniform are beloved by the people of Rwanda. Their institutions are among the most admired ones in the country, not only because of the wonderful peace, but also their active participation in socio-economic activities.

The most recognized of such activities is Army Week—an extraordinary effort from the RDF. It is really month-long, organized Liberation Day to respond to the people's high spirit of liberating themselves from diseases, hunger, poverty, and all types of oppression. Unlike other military personnel around the world, the Rwandan Army supports the community in their socio-economic activities.

This action of the RDF shows that Rwandan society has by far gone past conflicts for which it was originally famous. They engage in highly appreciated activities that include building schools and performing free medical services, which benefit vulnerable patients in remote areas of the country. According to local leaders, more than 20,000 people have benefited from the Army Week initiatives. Doctors in the military have offered free treatment to ophthalmology, hypertension, dental, and kidney patients across the country.

However, the heroism and patriotism of our men and women in uniform does not end with creating order and peace in their homeland. They have also been participating in our national priorities through keeping peace within the country and throughout the region. We have a brilliant contingency peacekeeping mission, in places like Liberia, Darfur, and Haiti.

Another outstanding thing about our peacekeepers is that they actively engage in open dialog with the citizens—keeping transparency at a very high level. They go beyond what is expected of them from the objectives set up by the United Nations, which are mainly to only keep the peace. Instead, they are actively working to make peace happen.

There is a huge difference between keeping peace and making peace. When you make peace, you initiate ways to reduce the need to keep peace. Peace has to be kept—because there is a disturbance, or you are trying to avoid a disturbance. When you make peace, you implement factors that will keep any disturbances from arising. In that regard, the Rwandan military has done an outstanding job, by extending Rwanda's vision to other nations in need. Rwandans believe that it isn't all about how the United Nations and superpowers make and keep peace for needy nations. It must be the active will of the citizens in a particular nation, wanting to make peace and knowing it's a desired state of development for their country.

The Rwandan Army deployed in the Darfur region, for example, makes peace by literally helping to build schools— they drill wells and help with getting firewood for women, so that they don't have to go so far to get those resources. This reduces the chances for women to be assaulted and/or violated while traveling to provide for their families. Before, women were constantly being assaulted; however, the efforts the Rwandan Army constantly makes play a critical role in safety. The Army improvises in ways that reduce the burden for women who travel many kilometers, looking for these essentials for their families.

These dedicated actions are valuable within our country, but the Army extends their generosity, culture and beliefs in whatever region they are deployed in. Ultimately, women in Darfur and the community in general benefit greatly from Rwandan integrity and cultural beliefs of self-reliance.

I honestly believe that the RDF was not picked as peacekeepers because of any massive resources or big numbers in their military personnel. Rather, I believe it is due to their history of being the most disciplined military in the region, coupled with the fact that they have restored peace and security in Rwanda in the shortest period possible, with minimum civilian causalities. They have kept the peace well, since the genocide.

It is due to their unwavering efforts that Rwanda is considered one of the safest countries in the region, if not the world. It is truly an honor for us to be able to be part of the global peacemakers and peacekeepers, after seventeen years of being abandoned by the UN peacekeepers. That is forgiveness in its purest form. We believe in peace, and we're willing to share what makes us who we are. The world is slowly starting to get our message: *we're the new hope of the nations.*

As Rwandans, we are proud of the men and women in the Rwandan uniform—both the National Police and the National Army. They are two of the most respected institutions in terms of fighting corruption, transparency, community policing, and making the people believe they are safe, secure, and protected. They are highly disciplined, working hard day and night within the community as protectors. We applaud and commend their noble work.

Rwanda makes it a point to recruit educated citizens, thus attempting to build their forces up with the smartest, most learned minds possible. There is a rigorous disciplinary assessment test required to join either institution. It is amazing to watch how much our Rwandan citizens trust their security. In general, the citizens believe that their security forces are there to protect them, not to fight against them.

These persons in uniform are also real members of our community, ones who have dedicated themselves to a higher national calling. We have worked hard to establish trust within the community, so we know that when people join the security forces, they are the same people we trusted while they dwelt amongst us. We trust them to do their job in protecting the nation's best interests, and we expect them to constantly be planning what they can do better to help the country move forward.

Our citizens also know that the National Army and the National Police are the same people that saved our nation from further genocide. It was their bravery, commitment, and heroism that have made us what we are today. They have truly earned the right to be trusted by the people; their services go far beyond "the self," orienting to "we," and not just "I".

Rwanda's Diaspora

The Diaspora of Rwanda plays a major role in the affairs of the country. They do more than contribute income and donations. They are actively involved in national priorities, the national agenda, building the democracy, the governance of the country—and so much more. Rwanda's leadership opens up forums so that the Diaspora can contribute and express their ideas about change, and offer their expertise. It does not matter where they reside in the world; our country values their input, and openly allows them to take part in the development of our country.

The Diaspora that left the country in 1959 has played a critical role in where we are as a nation today. Being in another land did not diminish their commitment to the nation. Many who have returned now have greater levels of education and expertise, gaining their educational advancements from the United States, Canada, Australia, the United Kingdom, and other African countries. We appreciate their positive influence.

The Rwandan Diaspora even initiated the campaign of building houses for orphans, famously known as the "One Dollar Campaign." Within less than a year, people had contributed four million dollars toward the related residence for orphans. The Government appreciated that the Diaspora reached back, and it duly helped. The Diasporans could've simply lived out a financially rewarding life in the countries where they reside, but their love of Rwanda compelled them to contribute to their homeland. Their dedicated efforts, along with those of many other friends and partners, have made the lives of orphans much better. Within their new homes, they will appreciate a sense of greater security and utmost wellbeing.

The connection between the Diaspora and our citizens is a deep one. We are bound by one tradition, language, culture, set of practices, and universal love for our country. No matter where we are in the world, the spirit of unity prevails among Rwandans. It is spelled out in our DNA! We're grateful to the countries that have hosted us throughout the world, but there is "no place like home." The heart of the Rwandan Diaspora is rooted in our lovely nation, well-known as "the Country of a Thousand Hills"—a home that's warm, bountiful, and far more than beautiful.

To summarize this section on our international relationships and the country's growth, Rwanda is constantly on the move. We have secured a plan, and that growing plan is helping us to do tremendous things for the country. We have gained respect from the international community, and have partnered with many different groups and organizations to help with the country's development.

However, our plan is not influenced from any outsiders setting their own agendas. Our plan comes from the people of Rwanda, is crafted by the people in their communities, and is a plan that is dreamed up by our Rwandan leaders. Only Rwandans and Rwandans alone contribute to this plan, for the nation and for the generations to come. We openly welcome partnerships only with those who value our plan.

We are succeeding because of each citizen's commitment to the cause of a better Rwanda. We have learned to put aside what makes us different from each other. We promote what unites us, and what makes Rwandans unique. We have learned to downplay our personal opinions on the leadership or the Government. Instead, we have decided to always do what is in the best interests of the country.

Through this commitment, our future generations will reap a thriving nation, a place of peace, unity, economic growth, educational wellbeing, and a greatly improved quality of life, because of all the lasting, real improvements that have been made by the current generation.

Section Three:

United We Stand

Chapter Fourteen: Patriotism and Heroism

Patriotism is defined as true love and devotion to one's country. For me, however, the meaning goes much, much deeper. It embraces the individual actions you perform for the good of your country, and encompasses the personal sacrifices you make in the best interests of its citizenship.

Rwandans show our patriotism every day, in ways ranging from comforting war-torn orphans to always speaking well about our country, even when things aren't exactly as we'd like them to be. In times of great need, we choose not to complain, but to support our beloved country. Patriotism is most deeply expressed when parents tell their children to love their country, thus passing patriotism on to the next generation. I still hear my mother's voice—filling me to overflowing with love for Rwanda.

Our national military sacrificed many of their lives to bring peace to our country. Today, the military and the National Police continue to put their lives in harm's way, for the protection of our sovereign country, and to maintain the dignity of our people. They are truly patriots. As I perform my life's work, I see so many people advancing the cause of our nation, and it makes me so proud.

Every day we are offered new opportunities to show our patriotism, and every day we can make a big impact on our nation—in our own personal ways. I greatly encourage everyone who reads this book to be patriotic, and help contribute to the success of our country.

It starts with simple things, such as abiding by the national Constitution, our policies, and the laws of the land. Patriotism is supported each time we choose to be concerned that every citizen has their human rights, we act with a moral conscience and share those values, and we protect our children from harm. It is expressed as we promote quality education and equal educational opportunities. It is also advanced as we support the activities that protect our precious environment. Patriotism is further supported when we speak up and are committed in everything we do to defend our values and our culture around the world. It involves always fighting corruption, and always speaking the truth.

Being patriotic means showing your appreciation for those who work tirelessly to advance the cause of our nation. It means exposing anything that would hinder the progress of our country. And most of all, being patriotic means getting involved with your community and leadership, whenever we as a nation forge new visions and dreams for our country, thus leaving an intact inheritance for our children and later generations.

For many centuries, there have been patriotic individuals in Rwanda who have been placed in the spotlight. However, the efforts of the ordinary citizen often go unrecognized. Those daily actions, even the small ones by ordinary people, have had a great impact on our society.

From a most tender age, it was imparted to me that *I was Rwanda,* and that Rwanda *was me!* When I was four years old, growing up in a refugee settlement in neighboring Uganda, I asked my father what Rwanda looked like—and he said,

"Rwanda looks just like you!" This was such a part of my life that it became the most natural thing for me to work hard on behalf of my country, and to sacrifice for the good of our country.

To me, the love and respect my mother taught me for Rwanda was in the most heroic of proportions. I am what I am because of her actions. There are parents all around the country today, doing the same thing. They are teaching their children to love and support Rwanda, and to get involved—to truly make a national difference.

None of their works should ever go unnoticed! Those parents have taught their children the honest family and community values, guided them with Rwandan wisdom, steeled them to be perpetually determined, and asked them to carefully make the right choices. All their efforts should be applauded. This is exactly how patriotism is lived out, on a daily basis.

We don't have to provoke bloodshed to validate our patriotism. Our country reconciled in the end without further bloodshed. That was a heroic and monumental task. Our citizens made a choice to reconcile with their neighbors, because it was for the good of the country to make that choice. In our reconciliation, we supported our Government and our communities. The very acts of rebuilding, showing our transparency, and using good governance are all true expressions of patriotism.

Patriotism goes well beyond our citizens. It includes partners and friends of Rwanda who've been ambassadors of peace and goodwill for our country, who've spread the message of our development abroad. In turn, we show our patriotism off as visitors come into our country, and we promote our Rwandan hospitality and moral values.

When we go abroad in international conferences and forums, we show our patriotism in how we represent ourselves—we hold our heads up, and *do not* allow our nation to be solely defined by genocide! Creating a global positive image is only advancing the cause of our Rwandan patriotism.

What I love about the spirit of patriotism is that it's available to all. It does not matter what the status or position of your life is. Anyone can act patriotically! What I would encourage our Government to do is begin to more often recognize the patriotic acts of our ordinary citizens, so that they will feel a sense of contribution, belonging and importance. This promotes unity, and will help our country become an even greater place of peace, honor, and integrity.

Also, the more patriotic that people feel, the better they feel about their country in general; they become even more willing to support their good, decent leadership. This is because patriotism invokes a sense of national pride, unity, and security. When national pride is awakened, people will want to do their best in everything that they do. This in turn creates a dynamically thriving economy.

Sometimes we can be rather narrow-minded in defining our patriotism. It's easy to think of people whom you see on TV every day as patriotic, or to think it's all about rich people making donations to the country, or the mainstream leadership, or those people held to be heroic for their wartime actions. We have a tendency to look up to these larger-than-life people, and then we cannot truly see our own patriotism.

We discount the things we do as ordinary citizens that have made our nation great. This has to stop! We need to open our minds wider, and view the bigger picture. Any act that an individual does, without any selfish motivation and for the good of the country, is patriotic. With that in mind, begin to look around you—and you will see that Rwandans are true patriots.

Leaders have a responsibility to make sure to honor the patriotic efforts of the citizens. I am speaking to all leaders, not just those in Government. This addresses leaders in churches, communities, schools, etc. If this is neglected and ordinary citizens feel that they aren't important, then they will not feel engaged, and that will eventually create animosity. It is in the best interests of the country to promote and praise all forms of patriotism.

Leaders must also duly recognize what patriotism inevitably does: it creates and fosters hope! When people are hopeful, they believe that the future is bright for their country. They believe that the efforts we put forth today will have a tremendous impact on our future. This is such a powerful force within the mechanics of patriotism.

Think about this: many Rwandans had spent 35 miserable years living in refugee settlements due to the dictatorship regime. Yet, their patriotism never diminished. They had hope. They believed that one day they would return to their beloved country—and when they did, that they would create a better nation. This actually came to pass. These were only ordinary people. That was an immeasurably powerful feat!

Patriotism also creates an atmosphere where citizens feel it is their duty to support and look out for their neighbors' wellbeing. This is done without selfish motivation, simply because it is the right thing to do. If I support my neighbor and my neighbor supports me, it builds trust. If I look out for my neighbor and my neighbor looks out for me, it builds security.

But who really is your neighbor? Well, the people you encounter every day are your neighbors—those living next-door, your teacher, your boss, your co-workers, your church members, your friends, and your family. Building trust and security has extremely far-reaching effects, because it creates peace. So in essence, patriotism is one of the strongest forces of peacekeeping.

Just imagine the type of influence you can be to your neighbor when you decide to live patriotically! As a child, I remember teachers who were patriotic. They believed in me, and wanted me to become the best person I could possibly ever be. Their influence to this day still guides me.

Those teachers are heroes to me. Many of them are still working. Their influence will never be fully known, because it is so far-reaching. The primary reason is that they made a decision to be patriotic. My daily prayer is that we will each do the same thing: be patriotic in our actions. What is your life's role—parent, doctor, teacher, contractor, or farmer? It doesn't matter. Do whatever you do with zeal, with perfection, and with proud determination to be the absolute best. *This is true patriotism!* There is so much power in each and every one of your good actions.

I want to add a word of caution here. There is much power in good actions, but there is also much power in bad ones. If you ever want to fail in your patriotism, then promote your bad actions. We have to be ever-vigilant as a nation in guarding against corruption and the failure to act properly. We Rwandans, of all people, know the destruction that bad actions cause.

The fastest way to bring bad actions to the forefront is to whine about, complain, and trash talk about the good that's being done. Not only that, but to complain a lot without being willing to come up with solutions as to how things might be improved. Rwanda has gone to great lengths to open up real public forums, so that people can contribute to the development of our country. But even with all of these mechanisms in place, many people only want to trash the country. In my opinion, that is the most unpatriotic action a person can shamefully engage in!

Unpatriotic people stir havoc and division. Patriotic people cause unity. It is your choice to choose your position. I have made my position clear, and encourage you to do the same. If you need everything to be absolutely perfect at all times and you have your own personal agenda, then I think you are only on the side of utmost havoc and division. But if you are willing to work for the good of all, even though it might cause you some personal discomfort, I think you are on the side of unity.

We need to remember that Rwanda—the scenic hills, the outspread land, and the beautiful lakes—will always be here. The primary objective we should be engaged in is making Rwanda a place to be lived in with peace and harmony. Other things may come and go: politicians, positions, jobs, problems, etc. These things are temporary, but the society that we leave behind for our future generations is permanent. So let's put trivial things aside, and do what we know is right!

Americans have this saying: "You are either part of the solution, or you're part of the problem." Really, consider who you are today. Know that it is *never too late* to be a patriot! Patriotism and heroism go hand-in-hand. They complement each other. I don't believe you can be a hero if you are not a patriot first. Just like a patriot, anyone can be a hero—any person who does something out of the ordinary.

Rwanda is filled with heroes. The amazing thing is that many Rwandans do not see themselves as heroes. They think that the extraordinary lives they live are normal. I really want to honor the citizens of Rwanda as heroes. I want them to see how great their heroic actions are!

If a woman loses her children, and then after the war picks up orphans so that she can be their new mother—that is extremely heroic. How is it that they found the strength and courage to raise an orphan after losing their own child? The deaths of children rank higher on an emotional scale than most traumas. In Rwanda, many women lost not only one child but many children, and yet they still reached out to orphans. Women all over the country have done that; we should honor them as heroes.

There are some women who have actually exceeded heroism, if that is truly possible. I am talking about the women who have taken in orphans from the communities of the people who had killed their children, or even more extremely, from the communities of their own sexual assault perpetrators. Can you imagine the strength it takes to do that? Those people are extra-special. They have reached a level of selflessness that many will never experience. Those persons have acted with a level of forgiveness and reconciliation that is vitally commendable. The stories of these people should be known all around the modern world.

The entire process of national reconciliation is heroic. The world truly has no idea what it took for the citizens of this country to stand up and say, "I forgive you" to the perpetrators and killers. Rwandans operated in mass forgiveness for the good of the country, despite their own personal pain and losses. We understood that unless we forgave, we would expose ourselves to the poisons of anger and hatred—thus rekindling the very forces that initially almost destroyed our nation.

Our actions to forgive dutifully lifted our own burdens. It caused us to change focus from our past to our future. It made us believe that if we could push past our pain, we would attain victory. That is an extreme effort! That is truly heroic. Our losses sensitized us, making us better people. We really need to see ourselves as heroes. I want Rwandans who read this book to be filled with national pride for overcoming extreme adversity.

There are even more acts of heroism that we overlook. How about exercising care and concern for a neighbor in need? You don't have to help them, but you do, not because you have to, but because you wish to express the goodness in your heart that exists, even after your personal losses.

Ordinarily, after a loss, people are consumed with their needs. What about people who share food when they barely have enough to feed themselves? What about people that give love—when they don't feel loved themselves? People who act that way give from the heart, powerfully and selflessly. We should all begin to recognize the heroism in these acts.

Every day, this goes on in Rwanda. People are constantly going beyond themselves. We don't know their names. We don't see them on TV, or hear about them on the radio or via other media sources. Yet all of these people are making Rwanda a better place. The next time you consider giving credit to the "patriots and heroes" you see on TV, consider giving credit to yourself, your family, your friends, and all the people whom you encounter that are making a difference.

It is the positive choices and small acts of kindness that we do which are making a world of difference in Rwanda.

Chapter Fifteen: The Influence of Patriotism and Heroism

If Rwandans truly begin to see the powerful actions of patriotism and heroism that they are expressing, spreading this message throughout the world, we can have a tremendous impact on other nations. If we can extend our message, no matter how small, it will assume an importance beyond our knowledge in other people's lives.

Perhaps you will tell your own Rwanda story to another person, write a book, make a movie, or invite someone into our country. All of these efforts make a significant difference. People need hope and inspiration. People in countries on the brink of genocide, who are experiencing it, or who are operating in gender inequality really need to hear our message, loud and clear.

There is still unbelievable suffering in African countries and other parts of the world, such as Afghanistan, Iraq, and the Middle East, South America, and many others. The levels of oppression are extremely high. The inequality of women and the disregard of input from the youth are overwhelming. *Hatred of their governments and their leadership is at the flash point!* But if we think globally, we can reach people with a message of healing before their countries erupt in violence, like ours did.

When I travel, I make sure to tell our story. I talk about the ordinary citizens who are heroes. I talk about the people who have taken measures to organize and hold their leadership accountable. I tell them how our country was ravaged, and yet now we live side-by-side in unity, peace, and safety. I let them know how our police and military have earned respect, and that it is possible to have law and order enforced without being violent.

These other people of a world in crisis can barely fathom that our police and military are friends to our citizens, and would never harm the weakest in our society, such as the children. These concepts are things that are often completely foreign to them. Yet, the message that I share offers them a renewed hope and vision for their own potential futures.

The reason they believe in my message is because they saw the near utter destruction of our nation. They know where we came from. They've witnessed our total transformation before their eyes. So, people of Rwanda, if you share your story, it will impact the world!

We are unique, and our suffering was extremely severe. There are not many countries in the world that can provide a message of hope, healing, reconciliation, and reconstruction like we can. Therefore, it is vitally important for us to see ourselves as heroes and patriots. We must continue to fight for what is right. We must continue to stand up and voice our concerns. We must be diligent to ensure that genocide does not define us. We should forever be defined by our patriotism and heroism.

Our patriotism must be fluid—it must move when we move. That means if you are a patriot while you're living in Rwanda, then if you travel you should keep the spirit of patriotism alive in your heart. We have a moral obligation to act without hypocrisy, because the purer our message is, the more impact it will have.

Patriotism is part of who you are, and you can exercise that each and every day. Every selfless act you perform as a citizen can be credited to your patriotism, and as you extend those acts by telling people your story, it will make a difference in the worldwide global society. *Never* underestimate the power of your life as an instrument of influence!

I sincerely wish to see the good that has developed in Rwanda continue for the next one hundred years—or even longer. I truly believe it can happen, as long as we stay unified and committed. The biggest enemy to peace that any nation can have is a self-centered population, including those harboring hatred and animosity toward their Government—and the Government toward its citizens. These were some of the major factors that ripped our own nation into shreds. I hereby reiterate that at all costs we must guard against that. We must realize that acting in self-interest often violates the rights of others, and that this can cause chaos.

I'm not saying that you should become totally selfless; of course, we all have the right to be "selfish" in some ways, to meet our own needs. I am stating that before you assert your rights, think about how it impacts others, because your most humble acts can have long-term consequences that either build or tear down our growing, thriving, beautiful nation.

If we intend to be ambassadors of peace, the image we display has to be a good one. That means if we are constantly displaying anger about the genocide, not only will the world see it, we will pass our anger down to the next generation. Negative actions such as those will only weaken our ability to influence people with our wonderful story.

As a whole, I think most Rwandans are better off now, because they value reconciliation. Nevertheless, it is good to be reminded about the dangers of anger, hostility, and the lack of forgiveness. We never want to experience our past again—and guarding against that will help to insure our future peace, giving us a healing message for other suffering nations.

Section Four:

Moving Forward

Chapter Sixteen: Becoming a Beacon of Hope to Others

We've come a long way, and we have a lot to offer other struggling countries. We've found secrets to coexistence that countries like Sri Lanka, the DRC, and Burundi only dream about! As we reach out to them, they too can learn how to reconcile and operate in peace. However, no matter how much goodwill we may bring to other countries, their people must actually want and work actively to change.

We have succeeded in becoming one of the best countries in the world in terms of economic growth, reconciliation, environmental friendliness, and many other factors—all because we keenly desired to see it happen. We desperately wanted to see change, and we unified to make sure we got the change we wanted to see. We developed our own ideas, and we learned from other successful countries about so many of the things that would make Rwanda much, much better.

We truly hope that our neighboring countries and other, more distant nations will do as we did. We are succeeding, and they can learn from us. One of our greatest triumphs is that we did this without using violence. We had a memorable share of it in the act of genocide, and we don't wish any nation to go through that before they come to terms with coexistence. Violence spreading from one generation to the next is destructive, and it doesn't help with promoting any forward actions to improve the country. It only leads to more conflict. If a country truly wants to change, then it has to be willing to put aside actions that have not worked historically, and begin to engage in new actions that provide results.

It simply boils down to making choices. You can choose to say that it's impossible for your nation to ever change, or you can choose to say that it is possible. People often hide behind excuses; they say, "We will never change, because our government is corrupt," or "Our government is so bad they cannot be reformed." But when people realize that any government's primary responsibility is to protect its people, and that the people really do have the power to make the government accountable, then things can change.

It all starts with speaking up. As mentioned earlier in this book, silence is what destroyed our country. We tolerated too much, and didn't raise our voices. However, once we stopped tolerating abuses and raised our voices, things have changed. Where there is unity, there is strength. We have a responsibility as human beings to denounce bad actions. We can't watch people in our community suffering and turn our backs, because if we do, in our time of need, there will be no support. As people become unified and denounce a bad action that is when positive change occurs.

The question we must ask ourselves is: do we have an obligation to reach out to our neighboring countries, and share our good news? Some may answer that question and say no, because we have our own country to maintain and our own problems to address. Others like me will answer that question with a "yes," because we cannot turn our backs—knowing that our neighbor is in trouble—and the more we erase their suffering, the more we become a better place in Rwanda, and so does the rest of the world.

We don't have to be absolutely perfect to reach out to other nations. For as much progress that we've made, we still have problems. But I believe that there is so much negative information being broadcasted in the world that any good information deserves a fighting chance.

One of the most suffering among our neighboring countries is the DRC (formerly Zaire). It strongly hurts my feelings to see that only a few kilometers across our border, women are brutally raped daily—while the neighboring country enjoys peace. I can imagine some critics denying this sympathy, pointing out to the DRC that Rwanda is a problem. In fact, some of the media of the world have claimed in the recent past that Rwanda is indeed the DRC's problem.

Yet, if we look deeper at this situation, we see the opposite viewpoint. On the contrary, the DRC was Rwanda's problem for sheltering many of the militia members who committed genocide, giving them safe haven in their country. We still have militias from the former genocidal regime which are hiding in the shadowed jungles of the DRC.

In my opinion, the DRC's government must step up to its commitment to its citizens and restore peace for its people. Rwandans are not responsible for the militias' presence in the DRC. We want them brought to justice. As for those innocent civilians who were recruited to remain in the jungles of that nation, they must follow Rwanda's campaign for military reintegration and come back home.

Hundreds of military members from the former regimes are now peacefully serving in Rwanda's own defense forces. But that is their choice to make. The DRC has the responsibilities for its citizens; so does Rwanda. There is very little Rwandans can do, except encourage the DRC to deny the criminals safe haven and to restore peace for its citizens.

I am not personally blaming or pointing a finger at them, and this should remain a personal opinion. I merely think that if the DRC wants things better for its citizens, it will have to deal with these problems in the best interests of the nation. I'm not implying that this is a simple task—however, being a leader is not a simple responsibility and you cannot accept it half-way.

As a nation which was hurt by the very people who enjoy safe haven in a neighboring country, we had ample justification for supporting our military to be in the DRC—for a period of time. As mentioned earlier, part of Rwanda's military responsibility was to rescue civilians who'd been taken by other militias, only to be used as human shields. It was also important to ensure that these militias were captured, or pushed away from operating in the border of a country that had already been severely harmed.

Irrespective of the truth around this matter, the media chose a different path when educating the world about the issue. The truth of the matter is that the militias are no friends of Rwanda. I think that my country does not regret the action of having been in the DRC. It worked for us. We rescued the innocent civilians held captives against their will, and hundreds of military personnel who managed to run away from militias came home, being reintegrated into the RDF. That is the true story, Rwanda's story about Rwandan affairs, one which the world should listen to.

But that was then and this is now—seventeen years later, when the DRC still remains in some confusion. We're neighbors; good neighbors in fact. We can help, but we cannot take care of it all for them. We can share some good practices of governance and legal system. We can even share some reconciliation mechanisms. As for the Rwandan militias still living in the DRC, they must be extradited to Rwanda, to face justice. In my opinion, Rwanda offers the best conditions for those genocide perpetrators, compared with a lot of other countries. We have what much of the outside world is missing: forgiveness and reconciliation mechanisms.

The DRC is darkly beautiful—not only due to its being one of the richest countries in Africa with mineral resources, i.e., gold and diamonds, but because it has the best greeneries and landscapes I've been privileged to view anywhere. Unfortunately, their densely rich forests make it somewhat difficult to round up perpetrators. However, attempting to do so would surely reduce the number of criminals currently disturbing the DRC's citizenship, especially concerning the atrocities done to women.

It is up to the people of the DRC to question their leadership and bring them to accountability. We can encourage our Government to work with the DRC until the criminals are forced out. We can also encourage our two countries to work together, linking their civil societies for the best practices. But the militias that continue the disturbances will have to face justice, either in the DRC or Rwanda. That's what our governments have their militaries for: to enforce laws and policies in place to protect their people.

There is suffering all around the world because governments have not gotten their priorities straight. The main goal of any government should be to protect its people. If a government cannot accomplish that, then in my opinion its leadership should resign. This may be a Utopian viewpoint to some, but to me it is a basic human right—and if you look through history, the main cause of any government's overturn hinged on its violation of human rights. Therefore, it is in any government's best interests to protect its citizens and make them feel secure.

Rwanda can become a brilliant beacon of hope for the DRC, Burundi, Southern Sudan, Darfur, Haiti, and many others. We don't have to wait for the European Union, the United States, and the UN to come to Rwanda, asking us to help those other beleaguered countries. We should reach out and feel their pain because we've been there, and do all that we can to alleviate their suffering. When they look to our country, they will see a nation to be respected because we support them, not envied when they so desperately desire peace and it is still far from them.

We should want them to feel the peace and security that we have. At the same time, they must want change enough to unite and obtain it. Coming to a peaceful coexistence cannot involve Rwanda imposing our viewpoints on their nation. Our role is only to support. They've got to make it happen. They have to ensure that their government supports them, and that the political elements creating corruption and insecurity are banished.

Rwandans are doing a great job supporting other nations. Our troops have been deployed to Haiti. They are providing many services there, such as cleaning the roads and doing construction projects. They also practice Umuganda (within a community support initiative) to help change their destiny—and they work hard in showing people how reconciliation is effective. Through these actions, Haitians are realizing that they don't need to wait on funding from the UN or the US to make improvements. They are becoming so empowered that they can develop their own country.

From my standpoint, as countries end their dependency on foreign aid, they also reduce their degrees of corruption. It is hugely important to address the foreign aid issue, and how it has the tendency to increase corruption. Foreign aid, if not monitored, directed, and used properly can actually cripple a society instead of helping it.

Corruption occurs when the contributions made on behalf of a country get into the hands of the wrong leadership. If it is a dictatorship or self-serving, those funds never get to the masses—and the monies never benefit their communities. As a result, money that was intended to build hospitals, improve education, and provide for the welfare of the citizens ends up as a channel of wealth and corruption for certain leaders. This practice of not accounting for these monies or reporting their use back to the benefactors providing them is the way that countries support dictatorship regimes without knowing it.

Despite our shortcomings, one thing that Rwandans in the 21st century can be proud of is that our leadership finally understood and applied the basic priority of security for its people, and has seen the good effects of uncorrupt governance. My hope is that we will never lose this aspect, and that it will continue for future generations.

My challenge to every Rwandan is to keep shining the light, keep doing good deeds, continue to strive for happiness, keep a bright smile, continue to develop the country, and continue to grow economically. As we continue with our shining deeds, we will have a glowing, golden torch to pass on to the next generation—a beautiful light which won't be diminished.

Chapter Seventeen: Mastering Our Own Destiny

Rwandans learned in the early days of the genocide's aftermath that we had to take control of our own destiny. We began making quality decisions for our country, eliminating outside influence—and this propelled us in the right direction. Truly understanding that we had to master our own fate was critical to achieving positive changes.

Within our plan of right choices, we chose to reconcile. We realized that holding a grudge or wanting to get revenge on those who wronged us served no positive value. It was in the nation's best interests to turn the page, start over, and move forward. This has been an extremely difficult and challenging path; we choose it because it was the road that would benefit future generations, produce unity, help us to coexist, help us tolerate each other, and help us live without discrimination.

We cannot stress the importance for other nations to see this critical aspect of our development. Every day, the positive choices we make advance our country. We are shaping our destiny daily by making the general decision to stay reconciled. We are looking for the best experiences in other nations, to adopt them for our own development. We are considering the best historical practices of our own country, and bringing them into the forefront.

We are devoted to doing our best work every day, realizing that as each citizen positively contributes in this way, our nation is continually benefitting. We are using technology to improve our position in the global economy. We are using education and employment development to boost productivity throughout the country. These are practices any struggling country can adopt, if they really want to see positive change.

Do you know why technology and productivity are such tremendous tools to use in reconciliation? They are important, because they make it possible to stay busy. When people are productively busy, there is no time left to commit acts of hatred against each other. I observed this while watching how westerners live. They too have their racial or discriminatory issues from the past, which often causes conflicts within their societies.

However, they are so busy working that they are too tired and spent to allow these conflicts to have preeminence. They would rather spend their time learning new skills and innovations, developing their material lifestyles with the purchase of homes, discovering and traveling, obtaining an education, becoming entrepreneurs, and purchasing needed commodities than dealing with those conflicts. That is a powerful life lesson.

Another factor westerners use to reduce conflict is to have the basic needs of their country covered: food, clothing, shelter, education, etc. When people aren't worried about their basic needs, it becomes easier to motivate them to seek more out of life. So many countries are in political turmoil, like the Ivory Coast, Zimbabwe, and Kenya, all because the basic needs of the people are not met—and this is causing continuous trouble. In order to move forward, something must be done to address the basic needs of their populations.

Once the basic needs are addressed, other development such as an advanced education, embracing technology, and increasing employment will follow. You cannot move forward unless your country is ready to invest in educating children. When those children become young adults, they cannot move ahead unless they study and graduate.

Once they do, jobs have to be readily available to keep them productive. They are thus encouraged to be innovative, and this spurs an entrepreneurial spirit. So, by creating a healthy basic needs plan, the cycle of productivity takes place.

Chapter Eighteen: Putting the Past behind Us

Any nation truly wishing to move forward must put the past away. It's disturbing to me as an activist to see that some of the dictatorship regimes in Africa have repeatedly done exactly what they accused their colonial masters of doing—which was to divide and rule the countries.

It is even more disturbing to see the same people whose parents or grandparents went through the "divide and rule" movement, and who've been placed in leadership positions, now leading with those same destructive policies. It perplexes me that the new leadership (once in office) would repeat the hateful practices which they've said they hated.

In most cases, people change leadership because they're promised change. Emerging leadership campaigns on a platform of "the promise of change." For the most part, some new governments do well in a limited period of time. But in most African countries, this does not last long enough, as personal interests start to overpower the people's interests. That is where divide and rule rears up, as the government starts to create factions among its citizens. They succeed by bribing one part of their citizens to be against another one. This creates conflict and destruction against the whole citizenship.

In my opinion, this is an awful shame. It causes so much discrimination within society, and no one truly benefits from it. Practicing the old forms of governance can only obtain old results from the former regimes: discrimination, inequality in the workplace, inequality in education, government powers not shared with the public, restrictions in business against certain individuals—and worst of all, restrictions in race relations. This latter is done to the degree that there is discrimination in national opportunities such as housing, land, public tenders, and more. Ethnic and political divisions are horrible practices that lead to destruction.

When people are busy and innovative, you rarely see any vivid ethnic divisions in accessing basic needs, except in rare circumstances. People coexist harmoniously together. It doesn't mean they do not have racial problems, but that they don't discriminate against their next-door neighbors. Why don't we do the same in our native cultures?

In Canada where I currently live, I don't personally know all of my neighbors—but at the same time, they don't bother me. Our neighbors live peacefully with us, no matter what different languages they speak or where they came from. Why can't we do this within our own countries, instead of discriminating ethnically or by tribe? Why do leaders in suppressive countries practice things that never benefited anyone in the past, nor ever will in the future? If there is to be any hope for the emerging countries, these actions must be banished.

I am extremely grateful that since the aftermath, Rwandans have decided to coexist. The classifications of Hutu and Tutsi have been removed. It feels so good for all of us to know that we are one people—*Rwandans!* We now share the same neighborhoods, have land in the same vicinity, intermarry, work together in the Government doing an excellent job, and are striving very hard to advance the country together. In our justice system, equal punishment is given—no matter the ethnicity—and guilty persons all serve in the same prisons. This could never have been attained under the older forms of our governance.

We shape our destiny by the things we do every day. We shape our future by learning from the past and avoiding practices that caused chaos. If every individual commits to reconciliation, then we will continue to grow economically, educationally, and through employment advances. If we all work together, we will build communities, health clinics, hospitals, schools, and new businesses. As our communities become far more literate, we will be more empowered to shape and plan for the future; we will eradicate poverty; and we will not need funds and input from western cultures that often come at unviable high prices.

When I look at the progress we're making in Rwanda, I see an understandably bright future, and the next generation is equally promising. Let's continue to support each other, to encourage our youth, and to reach out to other struggling nations.

When we look at where we came from and where we are now, can't you see the brilliance, joy and hope that lie ahead of us? Can't you see the beautiful country that we've developed for the next generation? I truly can, and I know that you can, too!

Section Five:

The Future is Bright!

Chapter Nineteen: Spotlighting our Future

The future of the next generation of Rwandans is wonderfully bright. They have inherited a clean slate from the current generation, making it possible for them to reach goals that would've been impossible for this generation. They are not entrenched in the hardships, pain, and reconciliation of the current generation.

Yes, our children have heard our stories; but their environment is so radically different from ours that they only experience "head" knowledge of the past, whereas the current generation has "heart" knowledge. It is a tremendous difference. You won't find the young generation engaged in conversation about our old problems. They are grasping the wonderful possibilities of an enlightened future, and are grateful that the present generation is building a strong foundation for them.

It is such an awesome reality when people of the current generation begin to relate the future to their children and grandchildren. Making thoughts of the future personal will help all of us strive very hard to leave them something of value. And as we work, we will leave them a shining legacy, a beautiful country, and a unified nation—safeguarded against our past.

We will leave a path for them to simply be able to live in peace, to dream and to experience the fruits of productivity. They will have the freedom to see the world through travel, and to bring the best concepts and ideas of other countries to Rwanda. They are engaging in technology light years ahead of anything our previous generation could've imagined. The banner that I envision this generation raising is one that states, "In unity we will succeed and make Rwanda a paradise." That is glorious!

The plan for this is already in place. Vision 2020 is one of the most aggressive, well-structured programs currently being enforced to lead the way for future generations. This plan is flexible, and whatever is not accomplished in the current 20-years plan will be added to the next Vision cycle. It doesn't matter how many Vision cycles are developed, even if it continues up to Vision 2050. The main goal is to plan and work for major accomplishments in each visionary cycle. Just imagine: many years in the future, the mere mention of the genocide and its aftermath will be fleeting, barely contemplated parts of our history!

Fifty years from now, Rwanda will be no longer considered as a developing country; it will be competing heavily on an international level. Can't you see it? Wouldn't you love to leave that legacy for your children's children? Well, open your eyes, knowing that each day we are building that foundation through proper planning—and we are setting matters up for that type of success. Take a bow, Rwandans, and applaud yourselves for overcoming the odds and shaping a bright future for all!

We are also molding the leadership of the future generations. Glimpses of this can be seen now, when people as young as ten are getting involved in politics and becoming concerned with the governance of the country. They see that we have rebuilt our Government. They know that the rules causing problems in the school systems are now diligently addressed, while making sure the prior era is not totally forgotten. They know the importance of maintaining good governance, and understand why the old system can never be allowed to resurface. Our future generation also knows the importance of human rights and the fight against anything that creates ethnic division. This knowledge being imparted to our youth creates greater security for a stable country in the generations to come.

What I envision is a country being democratically led by the youth, who are carrying the torch passed onto them by our present generation. I imagine our elders retiring with dignity and becoming a great source of guidance and wisdom for the youth. I see these elders being scholars, volunteers, and advisors—who are willing to contribute their knowledge, experience and goodwill for the best interests of the country—there will be no self-interests! This thought is a challenge to our normal way of thinking about how elders should become better leaders. The suggestion of their taking on an advisory role is certainly a new thought that is well worth exploring.

This leads to another challenging idea. Can we create a system of retirement for our elders? In many African countries and other developing nations, people don't run their retirement programs adequately. The governments take away their retirement contributions, which then land in the hands of corrupt leaders. Also, people don't know when to retire. No one is concerned enough to put the right policies on paper and explain them to the citizens. Some other countries plan for their seniors over 60 to have financial security, allowing them to give back to their community as elders. An elder's contribution is more valued than money, but we must want this to happen. I foresee that in future generations, progressive and productive ways to develop retirement programs will be implemented.

There is so much that can be gained from the older generations. I believe that the reason the young generation doesn't follow the paths made by the elders in most countries is because their leadership has failed—and they don't want to repeat their mistakes. But in areas where the leadership hasn't failed, there is much to learn. They have gone through challenges, dealt with problems, know how to resolve things with minimal conflict, and understand how to make realistic adjustments for the good of all.

Following this, Rwanda has embraced its elders, going beyond the current generation. Some of the same mechanisms that made reconciliation successful go back to the 1800s, when the monarchy and Rwanda's general structure brought people together. These are practices we should maintain. The ways of our elders may have to be modified to make them current to today's society, but there is great wisdom and value in their concepts. Those underlying guidelines set forth by the elders make us who we are, defining us as Rwandans.

I want to see the youth really embrace that wisdom, and truly understand that the cultural values that make us Rwandans are unique and cannot be easily copied. As our society expands and the youth have opportunities to visit other countries or be influenced by them, it's important to hold in high esteem the values and good governance of our country. You can learn great things from other countries, but never let that make you devalue in any measure the progress of your own country. You have to become a "hard thinker" to understand this—if you do not become a hard thinker, it's easy to be persuaded to do wrong by others.

For example, you might think: I want us to be like Singapore or Hong Kong. This is because you admire the advancement of those countries. It is wonderful to aspire toward the progress they're making, but you can't lose your national identity in this process. It is important that as we progress we keep the same moral values, the same cultural practices, and the same way of life. This will keep our Rwandan patriotism alive.

If we want to be so much like other countries that we adopt their ways, we will sacrifice the foundation that has already been built. We can grow like any other developed country, emulating a lot of the good we see from other societies, but on the inside we must remain Rwandans. Our values and our unique structure of governance are catalysts for growth, and we can never forget that. I implore our youth to always remember our roots.

Another word of wisdom I would like to leave for the young is for them to understand that there's a big difference between dreaming big and doing big things. Right now, there's a lot of zeal and optimism brimming from the youth. That is awesome! They have big ideas. That is wonderful. But the youth must realize that it takes a lot of work to bring big ideas to pass.

It is effortless to dream. You simply go to sleep, and see all your grand thoughts being played out on a large scale. But to bring those grand thoughts into reality takes dedication, perseverance, effort, labor, and intense motivation. You can continue to dream big—then you have something big to aspire for. But remember, doing big things is the real objective. When you combine dreaming big with doing big things, you get extraordinary results.

When I see many young people in Rwanda creating jobs to better the economy, getting involved in leadership, becoming activists, promoting equality, and fighting against discrimination in every area, I know the seeds of doing big things are already in place. We just need to continue down that rocky but travel-worthy road.

I applaud the youth for what they're doing. They have many more opportunities than our previous generations, because they can expand and know what is going on in other societies. They have television, the Internet, more education, and access to the media. They are not confined. They know about our country's values far more than the generations of the past. They have avenues of exchange and economy which were formerly not available to the civil public. This enables them to become sharp, and they are a very well-structured generation.

I personally mentor more than 1,000 university graduate individuals in different capacities. I hear what they're saying. They have big hopes and dreams. This is so encouraging to me! They want to see Rwanda become totally independent. They are not looking for some other country to help them. They want to be able to help themselves. I believe that concept alone will catapult Rwanda into becoming a realistically sophisticated and far more developed society. It will also bring a lasting, quality peace to our nation.

Another thing that will bring us even more peace and stability is the advancement of democracy. Not in the sense that most people think of democracy, such as freedom of speech, freedom of choice, etc. In some countries, people attend demonstrations defending their freedom of speech—when in reality there are important matters relating to food, healthcare, clothing, shelter, and adequate education that are left neglected. They strive so much to protect their concept of democracy that it is almost seen as something tangible, like something you can touch or eat. Can you truly live in a democracy with so many problems? To me, unless these problems are addressed, the concept of democracy is unstable.

According to *Webster's New World Thesaurus*, one of the purest definitions of democracy is "the greatest good, for the greatest number (of people)," and this is also defined by the word egalitarianism. When democratic nations truly begin doing the greatest good for the greatest number of people, then I will believe that they truly have a democracy.

But when you look around and see their tangled webs of problems, issues and inequalities which contradict true democracy, you might see that the focus should be on each person becoming more and more democratic. This means that they should contribute the greatest good they possibly can—so that all of society benefits. In baby steps, we're gradually doing this in Rwanda. I believe that if we continue to do this step-by-step, we will have a true national democracy in its greatest, purest form.

Our present generation has already laid the groundwork for the future generations. How has this been done? We have connected from the grassroots. We have developed a system of patriotism where the citizens are concerned for their neighbors. We have adhered to old wisdom that teaches everyone to contribute and work together. That's why we don't mind making everyone in communities responsible for building their own buildings, cleaning their own roads, beautifying their own areas, etc.

We have also rewritten the entire governing structure of our country, so that the voice of the people is heard, respected, and implemented. We have dismantled corruption. Also, we have laid the foundation of peace through forgiveness and reconciliation. Above all, we have leveled the playing field, making equality and anti-discrimination into major priorities.

The next crucial things we have done to set up a pure democracy is to make sure that the basic needs of individuals are truly met. This means continuing to develop an educational system that is available to all, bringing hospitals and healthcare to communities, addressing the need for food, and making sure that communities have clean water and electricity.

We are also developing new businesses—and the spirit of entrepreneurship is thriving. I can imagine the day when people are able to employ 5,000 to 10,000 people in their companies. Can you see that, too? When the people are content, when they have what they need, and when they feel safe from their government and their military, this is when a so-called democracy is truly a real, practicing democracy.

I want to see Rwanda entirely become a true democracy. We are working toward that in a realistic manner by taking care of our basic needs, and we are embedding within the foundations of our citizenship that caring for your neighbor and subduing any self-interest of greed and unlawful gain are the core of where we are now. The message I want Rwandans to get from this section is that we will surely become a true democracy, through our daily democratic actions.

Let's make sure that we live democratically—providing the greatest good for the greatest number of people that we encounter, every day of our lives. As we work hard to do this, then every good thing that a democracy offers will truly be ours, because we will constantly be making policies for the good of our nation. The freedoms that we structure in our Rwandan democracy will benefit all, because the people now had a voice.

The democracy that we build should also have a valid support system. In my opinion, combining wisdom, knowledge, and technological development will help to build our democracy. The application of wisdom in today's society does not seem to have as much clout as it should. But we should never devalue wisdom, because it dictates how we should act, giving us personal guidance on when things should be done, and discretion so that we will know when to speak and when to listen. It is truly a morality and virtue filter. Wisdom gives everyone and anyone insight. As you apply wisdom in your daily actions, it will guide you as to how to care for your neighbor, community, and country.

Knowledge is power—and a sound education enhances knowledge. It also helps you expand your perspective, and challenges your mind to grow, dream, and think big. We need a society that is flowing with literacy and advancing educational pursuits. If we have a solid education, it will help us to be able to understand and utilize technology.

Above all things, technology will revolutionize our country in ways never thought of or known about before. It is the critical element that will help us move beyond a developing country status more than anything else, because it has the power to move us forward on so many levels. All of the benefits that wisdom, knowledge, and technology bring add levels of contentment in communities—and that in turn supports democracy.

Chapter Twenty: Protecting Our Advancements

When I look at what the nation and especially the young people have done to develop tolerance, it makes me proud. Lack of tolerance caused the problems that we had. Tolerance overcomes those problems. The new Rwandan lifestyle is such that my own children don't know the difference between a Tutsi and a Hutu. *They look at people as people!*

They believe that as long as you go to the same school, live in the same neighborhood, and share a peaceful life, you can be friends. I can't see them losing their identities as they get older. Their upbringing has simply laid the foundation for peaceful coexistence. As they become future leaders, that mindset will also become embedded. All they will want to see is equal sharing in everything, because they see each other as equals. The building of tolerance has been a special and tremendous effort, and I would never in my lifetime or my children's lifetimes want to see it torn down.

In my opinion, there are a few things (if left unaddressed) that have the potential to override all the good we have done in building tolerance. I want to expose those negative factors, sounding a clarion call for our administration and the policymakers to take note and begin proactive measures to diffuse a potential threat. These factors are: (1) a potential wealth division between the rich and the poor; and (2) educational inequality, where the same educational standards aren't enforced in both public and private education.

We also have to make sure that healthcare is equal for all. If we allow a large gap between citizens in the categories, it will divide the nation and potentially cause worse problems than those that were caused by the ethnic divide. I couldn't imagine anything worse! I don't think any of us want the future generations to have to clean up anything that is so abysmal. They are inheriting true peace, and that must be well-guarded.

Imbalanced education also has the power to start a class society, with as much negative potency as the classes caused by an ethnic divide. We have to make sure that private school education and public school education provide the same and competitive levels of education. If private school students have a stronger edge, it will cause a divide. You shouldn't be able to distinguish between a child educated in the private system and one educated in the public system. Unfortunately, you can still see an imbalance, and that heads down to the neighborhoods where the children reside. We must develop fair and equitable standards for all students.

We as a nation need to begin thorough dialogs on this subject. If we don't, we are paving the way for our next generation to discriminate against itself, based on differing levels of education. This can be avoided if we plan now, developing incredible teachers and terrific school leadership for all educational systems—whether public or private.

The same thing applies to the division of the rich and the poor. We are a newly developed nation, and we have the chance to ensure that there is equality in the division of our wealth. We have gone to great lengths in our equality laws to help with this, but there is still work that needs to be done in the implementation of those laws. Now is the time to dialog. Now is the time to make sure that priorities are put in place to ensure that there is no wealth divide. As far as healthcare goes, equality is the key as well.

Chapter Twenty-One: Securing Our Future

When Rwandans begin to experience more of the "good life" in our own country, then there is less need to want to be someone else—such as Americans. What the current generation is doing is giving the future generation the foundation to want to cling to Rwanda. If we can make this place into one of the best nations in the world, with amenities like in the more developed countries, we will accomplish our greatest objectives.

However, right now our children are more content than those in our former generations, because they do indeed have some of the same things other countries have—and they can get involved through exchanging information, finding out things that would make Rwanda even better.

My parents' generation didn't have this ability, because they did not have a chance for broader education. That is also when the initial conflict was beginning. Our current generation is only beginning to experience these changes, because we have been so involved in cleaning up the mess that was left behind, and building a legacy for the future. But our young generation has a gigantic opportunity. They're enjoying a peaceful environment, a wide variety of educational choices, and feeling loved, appreciated and safe. They have us to protect them from harm—and our diligence offers our grandchildren a better way of life.

It's a bright, shiny new world for them, filled with places of discovery. The youth are the people we count on to push the agenda for 2050. Today's youth exchange information on the computer—because they understand technology; they share on Facebook, which can give them a global perspective, they're involved with social media, communicate using Skype, and they are able to travel and make new friends. I believe that this will increase exponentially over the next ten years, and I am so grateful to our generation for giving them that opportunity.

I wish our forefathers could've given us what we're giving them. But I am totally grateful for the gifts we received from our parents and grandparents. They deeply loved our Rwanda, and what they equipped us with is the knowledge to resolve our conflicts. Personally, I don't ever want to give my children or grandchildren a world they have to suffer through. I don't want them to have to be involved with how to reconcile after genocide and create a new unity. We really owe it to each generation to give them a peaceful and productive society, and not an oppressively chaotic and corrupt one. We are slowly but steadily doing that.

What I would like to see the young generation do is to take our visionary plan and make it work for the next 50 years or more. I want them to be free to do whatever they want that will bring good to our nation. This is our chance of a lifetime. Let's all continue to be diligent, paving the way for a great future for not only our personal children, but for all of the youth in Rwanda. We can give them a country so harmonious that they would never want to leave, a country so free that they are constantly setting their minds to making a better world for their future generations.

Think about this: if we work hard to ensure them a better life, what do you think will happen to our lives when we all become elders? It will be a place of peace. We can sit back and relax, knowing that the young generation will be operating a non-problematic society. We need to sweat with intense effort, now but not later, to ensure our nation of a beautiful future. If we fail to plan, if we fail to invest properly in the future generations, we are going to reap a less than optimal and perhaps even destructive future.

We above all nations know some of the harshest realities from the harvest of genocide that we reaped. Therefore, we must be most diligent to continue the phenomenal work we have done over the last seventeen years. We have built a new economy, and now there is a need to use it properly. We have to make sure people know what the economy is, and how to maintain it for the future. If we don't hand down corruption, there will be nothing for our youth to clean up. We must secure our future; failure is never an option!

The future generation is Rwanda's true renaissance. They are in a position to build any empire their hearts can imagine. They have the support of the people, and of the nation's leadership. If they are willing to work hard, they can build a family chain of 5-star hotels, restaurants, department stores, fashion dynasties, and super-sized businesses.

This opportunity is clearly marked and available. Our children and the children of extended generations will only have to maintain what has been built. So as each generation lives up to the societal charge given to them, the country will soar! Our generation was able to rebuild; their generation is to build greatness, and the next generation has a huge responsibility to hold allegiance to what has been inherited, to make it better.

Chapter Twenty-Two: Empowering Our Youth

What makes me extremely optimistic about the thriving future of Rwanda is when I look at the young generation, and see confidence abounding. They have so much belief in themselves, their country and their future. This is so opposite of what the current and previous generations had experienced. There was no possible way for us to develop any level of confidence, because we lived in fear, oppression, and death.

We didn't have any forces of society to help us build confidence. For example, education makes you confident; knowing that your country is working hard to give you a place of employment also builds confidence. Our generation struggled. Our parent's generation struggled more. Many of us (including myself) were raised in refugee camps and settlements, and we know the lack of the real confidence that education gives. Our parents gave us the best they had to offer, teaching us how to survive and hope. Our devastation left us so depleted that it gave us a powerful determination to give our children the security we never had.

In the new Rwanda, our entire group of children feels loved— even in the child-headed homes, where older orphans take care of younger ones. At the very least, they feel safe in their neighborhoods. The local leaders know them by their names, speaking for them in the communal meetings. Most of the older orphans take part in these meetings, to speak for themselves. Everyone has a voice in the new Rwanda. This vital attribute of our society makes me love my people even more!

In one particular child-headed home where I personally support girls to attend school, more than 230 orphans call me "Mummy". This is a great responsibility, one which I cannot turn away from. I do what I can to make each of them feel loved. I share Christmas dinner with them. I buy them small gifts that a child would need or enjoy for Christmas. But above all, I have fun, dance, and laugh with them. Many Rwandans do their best to bring laughter to these children. I encourage more people to do the same.

In brief, the young generation is much loved in Rwanda. They know the country believes in them and wants the absolute best for them. Every community is working hard to encourage and honor their dreams. They are so fortunate not to have guilt or shame from their previous actions gnawing away at their confidence. They can lift their heads high, and accomplish things we're not in a position to do.

You only need to open your eyes and look at the youth to see their confidence in excelling! They're getting involved, learning to speak the language of the world; they travel and are welcomed in places abroad; they're focused and know what they want in life; and they truly believe in an advanced education. They're not afraid to address tough topics such as teen pregnancy and sexually transmitted diseases, and they make useful contributions to the fight against HIV/AIDS— taboo subjects in my youth. Their dialogues on these subjects begin early, at around the age of 13. In doing so, they are learning prevention and family planning topics that will help their nation as a whole.

They have developed their own viewpoints on teenage pregnancy, which are completely opposite of the old generation. They don't believe that a girl should be ashamed, shunned, or penalized for having a child at a young age. Therefore, the old ways of putting them out of school—thus robbing them of potential advancement for their future—do not exist now. Supporting the educational opportunities of a young mother does not mean an endorsement of promiscuity; it means that the girl shouldn't be denied an education merely because of childbirth.

Modern educational opportunities also make single women more confident, because now they have choices. They don't have to marry young and immediately start a family. They can go to school, compete with the men, and develop their careers. They can build their own empires. In terms of leadership, this generation knows the Government structure better than any other (in my opinion) because they were raised in an environment in which communities demand leadership accountability. They were raised in areas that hold open forums, and they see the value of speaking up and getting your agenda in operation.

They are confident in their ability to see laws and policies enforced that benefit them because they engage in the democratic process. That alone is *hugely* mind-blowing! When the people know their power and know their ability to demand accountability from the leadership, the levels of public security and stability increases exponentially. These are the children that we have created with our souls. This is awesome beyond words.

Chapter Twenty-Three: Safeguarding the Zeal of Our Youth

We cannot afford to lose the zeal of youth. They are poised for leadership and productivity. Personally, I must voice the caution that we can lose that zeal if we are not very, very careful. The same generation that produced our creative and awesome youth is the same generation that could destroy it. The entire message of this book has been to show the advancements and sacrifices of this generation for the future generations—how our common citizens should be recognized for all their intense labors to restore the country—and to applaud them for setting a stage for the future generations to excel as never before.

I spend a lot of time with young people, hearing their questions and concerns. They are deeply concerned when they see the old generation clinging to power for ages and ages, even though the Constitution says otherwise. If your country has a constitution, you should respect it. This generation knows what is in their Constitution—you cannot blind them from the truth! They can look around the region and see certain members of leadership slowly attempting to minimize the Constitution for their own self-interests. But they trust their Constitution, and they also trust what their leadership has promised them; to betray that trust causes unforeseen negative repercussions.

Throughout this book, I have discussed the negative role that self-interest has played in our society. For seventeen years, we've worked to build unity and trust, and to weed out all corruption. I believe we owe it to our future not to betray that; I believe Rwandan leaders need to respond positively by doing what is right for the next generation. We will reap what we sow, and we can attain a paradise if we stay true to our vision, the Constitution, and the new ways of governance. We will surely reap destruction if we do otherwise.

There is a scripture in the Bible that says, "I put before you blessings and curses, life and death; therefore, choose life." If we are wise, we will choose life. Our nation will ultimately become what we make of it. If we hoard power, then the future generations will hoard power because that is the example we set. If we discriminate, they will discriminate. If we kill, they will kill. What kind of future do we want?

The other thing we have to safeguard is employment opportunities for the youth. This is absolutely critical. They are so excited about learning and advancing, extremely eager to complete their education and join the work force, or be in a position to create their own business. We must ensure we can meet those expectations. Otherwise, it will be like getting a package with your name on it, opening the box, and then finding it empty.

If we let them down in this area, they are going to question everything else. That will erode confidence. Once confidence gets eroded, then trust begins to decline. That is a dangerous, slippery slope that we cannot afford to have.

The other problem that may be created is an immediate brain drain. The current administration must with all diligence work on job creation. It cannot be mere talk. It has to be real effort, with results expected. People must make a living. The question we have to ask is: how badly do we want them to make that living in Rwanda? If we truly want this, then we have to do it. We have to meet these expected needs realistically.

This country graduates over 5,000 students a year; we need to offer them a 90% retention rate, due to employment availability. If we are only providing them with a 10% retention rate, we are failing both them and our country. We must take a serious approach to employment availability. It's not fair to people to work hard and come up empty-handed where it really counts—they must be able to provide for themselves and their families.

Rwanda's youth need to see their administration working as hard and effectively to create employment as it does when it's building schools, improving healthcare, and eradicating poverty. We must match the zeal of our intelligent, high-minded youth. We must also keep them busy in good, healthy labor. The nation rebuilt our educational system because we expected more from our citizens; let's give them a place to shine!

I want to see the young generation bring in tremendous salaries and have wonderful lifestyles. I don't want their dreams aborted. I want them to experience the reality of their dreams. They love this country, and its leadership loves them. Let's give them all what they need. Let's work tirelessly every day to not fail them in an area that's critical to their wellbeing and future posterity.

I'm confident that the Rwandan leadership is going to pull this off on a grand scale. We will be the envy of the region—if not the world—if we get this right. *I know we can do it!* Look at what we have already accomplished. It has all been quite remarkable. *We can do this!*

Section Six:

Dreams

Chapter Twenty-Four: My Rwandan Dreams

My dreams for Rwanda are immense, encompassing, and far-reaching—well beyond this generation. I hope that by my sharing my most precious dreams, you will begin to consider your own. As each of us live out the good dreams that we have for our nation, then our country materializes into the best country it can be.

Picture with me a society with a thriving middle class. The communities are all nearly spotless—they are colorful, clean, and beautiful! There is plenty of fresh, cool running water. Parents are happy and committed to their children, and the sounds of joy, life, and laughter ring loudly throughout the community, especially with the children.

Doesn't that sound like a place Rwandans could be proud of? Picture with me a society where there is no fear, no discrimination, and full equality at every level. I don't think that's beyond our reach—do you? We pressed the "restart" button on our nation, so there is nothing stopping us from building this type of society. We only need to expand our capacity to believe that we can accomplish our biggest dreams and wildest imaginations.

I dream of a Rwanda where citizens feel they have a moral obligation to take care of each other. In my mind, I envision a place where there are no orphans—in cases where the parents have died young. In my dreams, domestic violence or turmoil of any kind is not tolerated. It's a place where the leadership doesn't struggle to maintain power, but leaves office at an appointed time, legally and peacefully.

Does this sound like a Utopia? Perhaps, but isn't it better to plan and strive for good, than not to plan and get less than desirable results? The choices that we make determine the nation that we become. Why not put our efforts toward good? I want people to feel happy, to be fearless, to feel well protected in their country, and to feel that nothing can stop them from using their full potential and God-given talents.

I also believe in the sacredness of our ancestral heritage, so that as we become a more highly developed nation we will take our roots with us, and won't allow other influences to diminish who we are as Rwandans. I believe that we'll become so skilled at running our country that we don't have to look to any outside nation's influence. We do not need to be told what to do! We are big thinkers and can handle our own.

I envision a country where an independent lifestyle is greatly valued—people realize that nobody owes them anything. They understand that dreaming big and doing big things are the main factors determining your success. They understand that the only person responsible for your achievements is you—not your family or your Government. I envision a country where the people fully understand that hard work, application of wisdom, and self-empowerment through education give you the ability to create anything!

In my dreams, there's always full employment. Productively busy people are the builders of our nation. In my dreams, children are secure and well provided for; their young minds don't have to worry about any lack of provision, food or shelter—or about how they're going to survive. I don't want to see any child as the head of a household because their parents died of HIV/AIDS—or yet another genocide.

I want our children to enjoy being kids! They will have plenty of time to become real adults. Childhood should represent a special freedom, a time of extraordinary joy, and the ability to smile, laugh, and play. This is a time when they can afford to make mistakes, learning and growing from them. It's a time for them to explore, taking in everything freely from the world around them. Then when they are older (at least 23) and have gained mature understanding—let them marry and raise children. Families will be more nurtured, loving, and stable this way.

As I look around our country, I see Rwandan women who are absolutely gorgeous! But in my heart, I know that many of them don't feel pretty, comely or as lovely as they should. They can't feel beautiful, because the trauma of genocide has left them scarred, inside and outside. In those horrendous times, women's beauty was used against them—as they were made into targets of violence or rape. Other times, our women have been made to feel unequal, so that even as we work hard to reverse gender equality, the internal scars are still present.

Such a lack of self-worth has many looming faces. In my dreams, those faces don't exist anymore. Women are proud to be beautiful. Girls are proud to be pretty girls. They walk with confidence. They realize their value, their power, their potential. They know they have lots of choices.

I want to see them embrace marriage and enjoy parenting. I wish to see others who have chosen not to marry enjoy their single status—with no pressures to conform to the way things have been done in the past. I envision the day when all career fields are widely available, and there's nothing to stop them from becoming outstanding in their careers or enterprise. Women of high worth and men loving them for it, that's what I want to see!

As I've traveled around this world, I see how sports and entertainment unites countries. I really want to see our beloved Rwanda strong and united this way. Sports and entertainment make people feel as if they have no boundaries. The goal is simply to excel in your field, and bring a spirit of unity along for the journey. In those areas, people don't feel discriminated against. They co-mingle as equals. Healthy pride, strength, and goodwill are each expressed in the playing fields.

My husband plays golf, and his happiness increases every time he goes to play his beloved game. I love seeing him that way. I often tease him with, "What's the big deal about golf?" He knows I understand how it makes him feel great, but he will say back, "You have no idea how good playing golf makes me feel." That great feeling can be available to every person in the country if they begin to engage in sports with passion.

I want us to also develop in the musical arts. When I grew up, I loved to sing. My father gave me a deep love for singing. As a child, I would listen to him sing. No matter what was going on in his life, he had a song for it. Those lovely songs would lift his spirit when he was sad, or keep him encouraged when things were going well. Music in that sense becomes an important part of you.

I don't think I have the talent of a professional singer, but if I did, that would be my career. Singing makes you feel terrific— and has the power to unite so many people around the world. Perhaps when I retire I will write songs, giving them to professionals to sing.

Music and sports are vital to a good life. Such entertainment brings joy, happiness; it frees your spirit, gives you confidence, and helps you cherish who you are. We really need to develop the arts and sports in our nation. People need to engage in something more than work and making money.

In America they say, "All work and no play makes Jack a dull boy." They realize the importance of having national pastimes, and have developed their country around the performing arts, music, literature, sports, and other modern areas of entertainment. This is a very good quality we Rwandans can certainly learn from them!

Another dream I have for our country is that we all develop an awareness of environmental issues. I watched a documentary by Al Gore on global warming, and was shocked at how much I didn't know. One thing I took away from the program was that everyone has a responsibility to take care of the environment. Everything we do either makes our environment better or worse. We have control over issues like global warming and air pollution, and should become good stewards in those areas.

Rwanda is a relatively small, agriculturally-based country, and we have a dense native population that's steadily growing. As a patriotic citizen, it is my responsibility to relay a significant matter that will require both the support of the citizenship and the leadership. We all benefit when we have clean, pure air. If we pollute, we all suffer. We must consider how our purchases affect the quality of our lives, and live for a greener world. More cars on the road, for instance, mean more vehicle emissions.

Personally, I realize the impact of this and have decided not to purchase another vehicle, since my husband already has a car. This is a simple choice, but it will make a big difference to the air quality for this generation and all our future generations. When I stand on the balcony of my home in Kigali, take a trip to the village or visit the mountains, I want to be sure that I am breathing clean air. If we place a priority on taking care of the environment, then we will keep pollution at a minimum.

Chapter Twenty-Five: The Rwandan Way

If I could, I'd pay an archeologist to dig through the layers of time that the earth holds, and find out what makes Rwandans tick! There is something unique about us, distinguishable from any other people—I truly wish to discover its origins! We have such rich traditions, stories, and values. No matter where you reside in the world, those things don't change. I have a term for it: *Rwandanism*. It's truly the way we are.

For example, when a child is born it's cultural to gather up the whole community to bring gifts. But the most treasured gift of all is milk. It may sound strange to other people, but milk comes with vast significance in the Rwandan culture. What surprises me is that it doesn't matter where Rwandans live in the world—this practice still prevails.

We tell wonderful cultural stories and words of encouragement for the new families. This goes on everywhere a Rwandan family resides; it may be a community of four living in Toronto, or communities of 100-plus in New York, but the traditions carried out are the same as those in Kigali. Even more surprising, my children have adopted our culture—and they practice this even without my presence. They clearly follow Mom's footsteps. It is indeed imprinted in our DNA, right down to our milky bones!

These connections keep us rooted in our culture. It can be as simple as living in a foreign land—when all of a sudden you overhear someone speaking Kinyarwanda, our official mother tongue. I recall that in 1995, I was crossing the metro station in Amsterdam and a young man stepped in front of me, asking me point-blank if I was from Rwanda.

This should've been a startling moment—since this was right after the genocide. He may have been in the militia, and could've done me harm. But somehow, hearing his kind voice put me at ease. He was my countryman. We became instant friends; today, we are like relatives. Again, no matter where we are in the world, that special connection keeps us united and feeling at peace with one another.

Distance has not diminished this heritage. It's the same spirit—you can see it in our eyes. Whenever we live abroad, we want to connect to other Rwandans, unlike those cultures not proud of their roots, who would rather blend into the nationality of their new residence. We are close-knit. That's why it is hard to understand how we allowed the former regimes to poison us to the degree that we killed each other. However, the Rwanda of today is still the Rwanda of yesterday—that is, before the "divide and conquer" regimes. That was and is simply a wonderful place!

Our modern Rwandan culture is embedded with good qualities. For example, the men won't eat unless the children have eaten, because they realize that children need to be nourished more than adults. Our men also really have a high level of respect for our women; they treat them like queens, and their daughters like princesses. Men will not even sit in a seat before making sure that every woman has a place to sit. Yet another unique tradition is the honor of the birth order. The last-born child is significant in the culture, and is celebrated. I am a last-born, and know the deep honor bestowed upon me by my family.

And our history shows the strength of our women, who have always held leadership positions. Rwanda has recently made gains in the field of feminism—as I previously stated, it was voted in 2011 the second-best country in Africa among Commonwealth countries to be born a girl, and the 10th such nation in the Commonwealth. Rwanda also scored 'A's for female political participation, its fertility rate of girls aged 15–19 years, and its gender pay gap. That is a huge honor, considering the oppressive treatment of women in other African countries and beyond.

Personally, I've never regretted being born a woman. I would do it all over again if I had to! Because I come from a culture that puts value on women and treats its children equally, it wouldn't be a problem. I have truly gotten tons of love and respect from my father, brothers, teachers, and neighbors. My husband has never questioned my capabilities. My son calls me the brightest woman he has ever seen. Isn't that a great feeling—and it can be available to any woman who lives in a country where women are highly and wisely valued.

I never want us to lose those good qualities. Recently, when I heard (through speaking with the police and certain women) that there were issues of domestic violence in Rwanda, I was appalled, thinking: how could it be? I realize that change through each generation takes place, mixing of cultures occurs, and that some ways and traditions must inevitably age; but domestic violence is a complete departure from our heritage of respect for women and the living of a dignified life. Surely we cannot allow this evil to filter into our peaceful society. That would be anti-cultural and destructive, and would alter the nature of who we are!

Meanwhile, I am not implying that our families have no problems. They occur daily at every level, and are part of life. People can have awful, irreconcilable differences, but domestic violence shouldn't take place. Violence against the mother of your children only traumatizes the sons and daughters you cherish. This behavior is not the Rwandan way.

We are a kind, loving, supportive, forgiving, and reconciling people. Our men deeply love their wives and families. We need to always be who we are, and abandon any form of domestic violence. I implore any person reading this book who is engaged in acts of violence—*STOP!* We need to return to the days of treating our women like royalty, our sons like princes and our daughters like princesses.

Our Rwandanism is also seen in our resilience, patience, and hope. If it were not for our resilience, the country would've vanished long ago. People would have given up, assimilating into the next region or country. But since 1959, there's been a strong patriotism and determination that we would be Rwandans once again. As a result, we are not merely scattered throughout the world. We have a homeland. We have a culture.

People from other countries look at us and can't understand our strength. They don't realize that deep within our heritage is the undying spirit of hope, and that it keeps us moving forward, from crying and caving in during the most heinous of traumatic circumstances. We have a saying, "Who do you cry for, when the person is already gone?" We don't look back—we look forward. We bury our dead and honor their lives by living a life they would be proud of.

As I see it, writing this book brings a smile to my mother's face. Even though she is gone, she watches over me and my family with joy. I have become the woman she wanted me to be. She still expects much more from me, and I will do my best to pass it on to my children. I believe most Rwandans feel the same way—every mother from Rwanda, dead or alive.

Our Rwandan expression, "We hold the right breast to bless the nation" still exists today. A true and loving idea, it is much, much stronger than any mere political power. It's our way of connecting with our ancestors, and it honors their unforgettable guiding wisdom.

Speaking personally, I haven't had any time to cry. When those flaming memories surface of my loved ones who perished in the war and the terrible genocide, I know that I must move forward, always walking in forgiveness. There is hope for anyone who asks to be healed. Through my prayers and meditation, I see their faces and know they wouldn't want me to cry. They want me to be the best I can be, and honor their lives.

I know they'd be tremendously proud of me. Every day I try to make their memories shine. My hope overrides my pain. We Rwandans appreciate their hard work, which earned them respect. Our parents, big brothers, and big sisters worked diligently and courageously to earn that respect, losing their lives and their dignity at times for the sake of community and sibling education.

Also, some individuals and leaders in neighboring countries went out of their way to risk their lives and political careers to help Rwandan refugees and their children. Some countries like Uganda, the DRC, Burundi, and Tanzania are greatly appreciated at particular times, when they treated Rwandans with great respect after the recognition of our hard work, knowledge and skills. However, our suffering when others treated us inhumanely just because we were Rwandans will never be erased from our history.

Multitudes of our citizens lived in refugee camps (some are still there) in West Africa, East Africa, Central Africa, the Great Lakes region, and many others. We were treated like scum and harassed; we were fiercely discriminated against. Due to political turmoil in their host countries, the Rwandan refugees of 1959 not only suffered the harshness of being refugees, but also became the victims of heated political battles.

People had to survive cholera, dysentery, and the tsetse flies, and many people died in those dark days—particularly women and children—because of malnutrition, starvation, and tropical diseases. Suffering by some of the Rwandans in Zaire (now the DRC) included that they were put on planes and thrown into the tropical forests by the Zairian Government.

The suffering of Rwandans who lived in refugee-confined villages in Mushiha, Mugera, and many other areas in Burundi, holds a lot for them to tell their children and future generations to come. However, this really only made them stronger, bringing them together as Rwandans living outside their country. Their solidarity was extraordinary.

They even managed to build schools for their children. St. Albert is a famous secondary school that became popular in Burundi's education system, even though it was built by Rwandans as a result of their children being discrimination against by the Government of Burundi. Its original name was "Impunzi/Refugee School."

The Rwandans in Tanzania not only suffered a great deal as refugees, but also from the undeveloped nature of their host country. Tanzania was a relatively less developed country compared to the rest of East Africa. It was impossible for their own citizens to access their basic needs, let alone our refugees being able to do so. Due to the hard work that is embedded in the Rwandan blood, the people who lived in Karagwe, Kimuli, Nkwenda, Cyabashaka, and Muyenzi of Tanzania went on to settle and deal with the hardships by doing what they knew was essential for survival—raising cattle and keeping the land grazed.

Fortunately, these Rwandan refugees managed to survive, later starting to develop some abandoned villages in Tanzanian territories on their own. But sadly, they were reminded constantly that they were only refugees, and that they should go back to their country and leave everything behind to the Tanzanians.

History will also never forget the suffering of Rwandan refugees who lived in a variety of political turbulences in Uganda. Confined in the refugee settlements of Nshungerezi,

Nyakivala, Gahunge, Cyaka, and Cyangwari, they were unable to freely move in and around the country. This generation of refugees suffered the most—due to the unrest of the political regime. For those who attempted to assimilate into Ugandan free communities such as Masaka and Ankore, they became scapegoats for many governments seeking or losing power.

A few people who made it to Kenya endured the same fate, unless they had enough money to bribe officials (mostly the police) on a regular basis. Most young men were subject to be imprisoned by the police, without justification. Almost all Rwandan refugees who lived and were born in Kenya never obtained any form of identification—only Refugee ID cards. These cards were not sufficient for those trying to obtain education or employment.

Meantime, those Rwandans who by default or circumstance remained in Rwanda in the bad times were harshly oppressed, under the bad regimes. Some lived in fear, and others were without freedom of expression unless they sided with the governmental wrongs. From 1959–1994, Rwandans within Rwanda were discriminated, oppressed, imprisoned, and manipulated. Their silence became their tool of survival.

Nonetheless, this suffering from those earlier times became a blessing in disguise. Rwandans started to use common sense, uniting to support the RPF—liberating themselves. But as in the American expression, it was mainly a "doomed if you do, doomed if you don't" situation, due to our turmoil and the genocide.

At any rate, suffering or no suffering, as a culture we have chosen not to repay evil with evil. In the new Rwanda, the same people who have wronged our country and its citizens have come to us and sought residency. Our Government has allowed them to come. They have been allowed to do business; everything is peaceful for them. We do not call them names. We see them only as friends and partners. Those who admire us have become citizens—with no strings attached. That is the Rwandan way! We can't explain it to the world; it is merely the reality of who and what we are. It's an enigma that we could do this after being mistreated for 40 years, but it simply comes down to understanding Rwandanism.

We refuse to take revenge. We will not allow ourselves to be poisoned by others' problems—they have to be addressed, and the perpetrators are held accountable to God for their evil. As far as the nation is concerned, if they want to live in Rwanda (it's the safest country in the region), and they want to thrive in our society and start new businesses, they are welcome. It may serve as a reason for them to learn respect and dignity here, and return to teach these things to the people back in their own countries. We will look upon them with the same respect that we have for our own nationals. I applaud our Government for their actions in this area.

As a result of our ways, we have been misunderstood, miscalculated, and misinterpreted. We have been abused in the media, where people have written against us, harboring malice. They may say or do what they will, but we won't be moved from our dignity of life and our cultural values that dictate how we respond. We will overcome any oppression—and the world has already seen us do it masterfully before.

My father and grandmother put it this way, "No matter how hungry you are, you don't have any excuse to steal." We calculate our responses. A Rwandan would rather starve than steal. We will go days without food, until someone offers us a meal we can eat with dignity. We value our reputations, and won't react when others attempt to tarnish them.

I have heard people from East Africa say, "Those Rwandans are resilient. They can be poor, but they will look clean; they may be hungry, but you would never know it." Our experience has taught us to stay controlled, hopeful, and resilient—in doing this, we will survive anything.

Chapter Twenty-Six: Will You Share Your Dreams?

I hope that by reading this book you've been challenged to dream big and do big things. I hope you've also been inspired to put your mind, heart, prayers, and labors to good use—in such ways that your nation prospers. I have exalted the citizenship of this country for the tremendous efforts you have made to rebuild our country and reunite our people. Your next call of action is to continue, to never stop believing in our national ability to be a major player on the global scale.

Now is the time for you to lift your voice, to speak your dream throughout your community. Now is the time to make your dream a reality, to believe in yourself and soar high! Now is the time to plant your vision into the minds of your children, and teach them to dream big and do big things.

To encourage your efforts, I've spoken with Rwandans and friends of Rwanda from around the world—asking them to share their dreams. They did this without hesitation, because they understand the power of inspiration. I'm sure that after I write this book (and more beautiful changes impact our nation) that I will be doing revised versions, so feel free to share your dreams with me so that they can be added to the next book.

This book is truly for the people, and like these individuals, your input is invaluable. Again, I hope you are truly encouraged and inspired by these voices of our people and our good friends.

Chapter Twenty-Seven: Dreamers

Beautiful Dreams for Rwanda:

- *"The Rwanda of my dreams is a country where sustainable development of her citizenry is achieved, where the population is educated and computer literate, where good governance principles are the guide of Rwandan leadership, and where foreigners come and learn from our experience."*

- *"A strong self-sustaining economy driven mostly by the private sector and a strong middle income, a strong political base supported by a Constitution that makes it hard for one single level of Government to enact laws. Here we can take as an example the Constitution of the USA, which for over 200 years has been enacted only ten times. Any change should be debated from the grassroots level up to Parliament, without political influence. Based on the history of Rwanda, I would love to see Rwanda where Rwandans live truly in harmony, where nobody wishes harm on the other (of course, this is Utopia), but that is my dream."*

- *"My dream for Rwanda is a country where every citizen will feel at home better than anywhere else, where the right to life and all fundamental rights will be respected for all, where core values will be the motto, and where the pride of being Rwandan will enlighten our youth's faces."*

- *"A dream for Rwanda in my head is that everyone has the opportunity for self-fulfillment. That people have a dream of themselves in a worldly sense, meaning that they feel they have a place in the world, and the world has a place for them. That they have achievable ambitions that are not restricted to earning money and surviving, but include for example traveling because they can, or being respected artists, architects and engineers because there is a demand for their creativity someplace in the world. That they have a desire to learn about things that are not directly related to themselves, such as Japanese calligraphy or South American capybaras, and this has meaning to them. In effect, they are engaged in the world at large."*

- *"I dream of Rwanda to be one of the developed countries in the next 20 years, a country that will be a role model for many in terms of democracy, economic development, human rights, a hub for gender equality...and social development (health and education)."*

- *"My dream for Rwanda is a successful country in the region, a middle income economy proud of itself and confident in its leadership, and an un-leveled developmental agenda achievable within our own means and minimum external influence, A Diaspora proud of its roots, out to challenge the ill-intended and convincing to skeptics, the ability to lure investors and encourage all Rwandans to feel secure—both at home and in the Diaspora."*

- *"My dream for Rwanda is a country that is safe and secure for Rwandans and non-Rwandans, and their property. It should have food, security, and offer job-working opportunities for all its citizens to earn a decent income/living."*

- *"My dream about Rwanda: in the next 20 years, I am looking at a city with all roads constructed (even those in the suburbs), trees* grown and taller buildings constructed in the city center. However, I see great traffic jams in the next few years! I dream of a very peaceful country, whose laws and policies continue to be strictly followed, and becoming a regional hub, a model for a number of things! AMEN! I dream of a country whose women are truly empowered and are making strides to change other women in the region."

- "My dream for Rwanda is to see one day when no more women die when giving life. The journey is still long, but we shall get there where in Rwanda, maternal healthcare shall be a model experience."

- "My dream is to see a united and secure Rwanda, a safe haven for its entire people, with every child educated, every woman/man respected, and every minority of any kind given opportunities to succeed. A country with systems that cannot be easily broken regardless of who is in power, a Green Rwanda where trees, lakes, rivers, and animals thrive because they are protected, a country that will carry the flag of peace to show the world that peace is possible regardless of the pain endured and the challenges faced in the past."

- "I dream of harmony, peace and prosperity for all, where everyone is valued, allowed, and empowered to contribute to the development progress. A reconciled and dignified people with a stable and sustainable democracy firmly planted in our unique cultural identity."

- "To see Rwanda developed in many and different domains: industry, education, healthcare, etc. I want to see all services *computerized in a bid to limit and eradicate corruption, and a country where people are determined with a passionate interest in business—and striving professionally."*

- *"My dream is that one day all Rwandan citizens will be able to feed themselves without any sort of assistance from abroad."*

- *"My dream for Rwanda is seeing it becoming a famous country in Africa and in the whole world in terms of stability and economic development, also seeing Rwandans living in harmony without seeing themselves in ethnicity like Tutsis, Hutus, or TWA— instead, working together as Rwandans to develop our country. And I am eagerly striving to be a part of all those changes I wish for Rwanda (Impossible is Nothing)."*

- *"My dream for Rwanda is to have it get rid of all poverty and economic inequalities that it faces, and it should loosen up a little its business politics, which seem a bit harsh and which don't favor the middle class. I want to have it focus more on the education of its youth and less on politics; finally, I dream of an everlasting peace in this country."*

- *"My dream for Rwanda has always been to be liberated from all types of divisions, neo-colonialism, and backwardness like genocide ideology and self-seeking politics. Only unity and self-respect coupled with hard work will save Rwanda from its evils—(which are) mainly occasioned by colonialism and parmehutism."*

- *"My dream is to see Rwanda becoming a respected country in Africa in all aspects of development, with a number-one rank in culture in Africa—and to see every Rwandan be proud of being Rwandan and having patriotism for his country; for my side, I want to clear my way by using the opportunities that we have and working together with my colleagues in order to give our contributions to our country."*

- *"My dream for Rwanda (is to be) without a genocide ideology, especially in young people, when being a Hutu or Tutsi will not be a problem to your neighbor. I salute the effort of our Government in this respect in particular and in unity and reconciliation in general, but I still think we have not yet reached the ideal situation."*

- *"My dream for Rwanda is that one day the gender balance will exist where agriculturalist women give ideas and make the decisions on agriculture production, on agriculture techniques, and on income sharing in family needs."*

- *"To see Rwanda stay on the right path that makes us today a role model for other African countries and keeps the focus on our Vision 2020 by initiating good partnerships and building trust with strong business relationships."*

- *"My dream for Rwanda is to be a secure and a developed country, where everyone will be proud of being called a Rwandan, where reconciliation will be achieved a hundred percent. I'm dreaming to have no discrimination based on any facts."*

- *"My dream for Rwanda is security for all, eradication of poverty, employment for all Rwandese able to work, and access for every Rwandese to education and healthcare—and continuous development."*

- *"My dream for Rwanda is to see it really meet its Vision 2020 and be truly the Singapore of Africa it so strives to be. I would like to see Rwanda being the destination of and prestigious nation for African elites in terms of development and culture. Believing in that dream is soon to be a reality. My dream and hope is that Rwanda will continue to perplex the minds of those who wish it ill, by proving them wrong—especially when it will reach the stage of 100% self-sufficient."*

- *"My dream for Rwanda is to see it becoming a paradise country."*

- *"My dream for Rwanda is to see Rwanda move from (the category of) countries in the process of development to developed countries."*

- *"My dream for my country is political stability and democracy, maintaining our economic development and growth."*

- *"I dream of a better Rwanda, better in such a way that there are better education systems and our people to be more educated, for education to be available to everyone. Because I believe education is the solution to most of the problems that we have today in our country, be it directly or indirectly. Of course, not forgetting more peace and prosperity; this in one way or another depends so much on education. So, in a few words that is my dream for Rwanda— a more educated Rwanda."*

- *"My dream for Rwanda is to recover fully from the "dark" past, with total integration and reconciliation of her people, visible social and economic development, and overall peace and security, with an open door to a political platform for all democracies."*

Rwanda's Realized Dreams:

- *"I love the country's achievements, especially in terms of security, an enabler of quick growth in investment and development."*

- *"Rwanda is honestly President Kagame's leadership, notwithstanding that every person has their own weaknesses, but he has steered this country from the ashes of genocide, managed to have the country reconcile with itself, and achieved economic growth that only needs to be sustained."*

- *"I love the peace that prevails in Rwanda—and most of all the resilience of Rwandans after the genocide. This indeed is a good omen for a better Rwanda, and non-Rwandans fail to understand it. I love the spirit of Rwandans."*

- *"I love the democracy in Rwanda, the quick steps taken in terms of development (recovery). I love the current Government programs and above all, the special attention given to doing business in Rwanda as well as the promotion of gender equality."*

- *"I love the resilience of the people and their sense of hope. I love their sense of a future, without clearly knowing what it may be. I love the way they get up in the morning and work at something in the hope that it leads to something better. Their persistence, their creativity and problem solving, their hard work and their sense of fun. Their ability to sing endlessly and dance until they drop, and how a smile never leaves their faces. Rwandans know so much about what life is all about. They have an ability to assimilate the new into the old and make both richer, without losing too much of their past as they move forward."*

- *"I love Rwanda's coherence and homogeneity; it's small as country geographically, but big enough as a nation-state, with a people that is automated by the national cause toward a desired common destiny. Pride in self, individually and nationally, excellent, dynamic and visionary leadership, cherished and clear national vision that rightly blends with the MDG."*

- *"The indestructibility of Rwandans is amazing! Look at how they have bounced back after the 1994 Tutsi Genocide, and the humiliating and harrowing refugee life some of them lived for 30-something years. Rwandans are a resilient people, very determined wherever you throw them, despite the odds. The greatest asset Rwanda has is its people, and this is what I love most. Secondly, I love Rwandan culture—the dance, the poetry/imivugo, the history (the good parts).*

- *"I love the climate; I love the cleanliness of Kigali and our other cities. Last but not least, I love our leadership that is focused and doing everything possible to facilitate acceleration of the socio-economic development of Rwandans. I love the imihigo/performance management contracts and the way they have brought local leaders to account."*

- *"I love the Umuganda, the cleanliness of the city, the peaceful nature of the whole country. I love the healthcare (Mutuelles de Santé). I love the Parliament full of women. I love the courage of all the leaders, who work with a feeling that "All eyes are on me," so that they are effective and have a feeling that they have to work for the people. I love the green nature of the country, the hills."*

- *"I appreciate the political will of the Government to support women to live a decent life. Today, I feel more proud to be born female, because I believe without doubt that my society accepts that I have capabilities like those of my male counterparts. I can access education, choose a career of my choice, can be listened to, and my active participation in decision-making positions is guaranteed the moment I show interest and capability. And where I may be discriminated (against), laws are there to help me seek justice. No one demeans me anymore because I am a woman."*

- *"I am proud of the wise leadership we have. I appreciate every effort made by our current Government—putting in to set up the trend that has jumpstarted development and social justice. I love the collective spirit most Rwandans have to forge ahead and not allow our past to stop us from going where we want to be. I dream when Rwanda will have social services that really work, and that all Rwandans can enjoy social benefits like in developed countries. I love the peace Rwandans are enjoying."*

- *"I love our people, I love our uncorrupted culture, songs, dances, poetry, and our humanity—(Ubuntu/Ubumuntu) is stronger than our animosity."*

- *"I love Rwanda's leadership and politics, which don't expect to benefit only one group of Rwandans, but (involve) all Rwandans being given the same chance in all fields and treated in the same manner. I do love also the young Rwandans, who are ambitious to develop their country—and most of them want to be part of it to happen. (I appreciate the commitment of Rwandan leaders and Rwandans in fighting against any ethnic-related discrimination), I hate so much anyone who may promote or inspire any form of discrimination among Rwandans. United we stand!"*

- *"I appreciate its uniqueness, its capacity to solve its own problems (homegrown solutions), its beauty, its soft power, its diverse people with experience from all over the world, its unique culture."*

- *"I appreciate how our President loves the Rwandan people, how he always thinks about their development and the accountability day, where the authorities must explain their activities to populations, and how some people work hard for the development of others, just like Justine."*

- *"What I love most about Rwanda is the vision, the patriotism, and the integrity of some of the leaders, the courage, the dignity and the kindness (urugwiro) of some of the Rwandese, the leadership of Rwanda—and I love the beauty of the country."*

- *"What I love about Rwanda is the fact that I understand and feel understood (there). Rwanda gives me something I can never get anywhere (else) in the world, which is a sense of belonging, visibility and hope. Rwanda is the resiliency, self-respect, and dignity of its people—minus the bad apples. They live like kings in their little castles, behave like royalty; (the rest of us) always strive for a dignified life despite adversities."*

- *"I adore the equal opportunity in education, and in employment I adore also our justice and security, and our cleanliness."*

- *"I love our climate. The population is sharing one same language, (it's a) small country, easy to handle, the population is ready to obey and to serve the nation, Availability of huge natural resources."*

- *"I love the potential of the people and the country as a whole. Rwandans have so much potential to grow and to be better, I mean just as much as other countries; but Rwanda seems able to maximize that potential."*

- *"I love our President, the beauty of our people and landscape; Rwanda is also blessed with a rich traditional and cultural heritage that not only attracts her inhabitants, but foreigners as well."*

Chapter Twenty-Eight: This is Your Time, Rwanda!

This book was a most wonderful journey for me, and I hope it was also an enlightening one for you. If you are from Rwanda, you should be much prouder now of what that means to you—and more determined than ever to make our country into a Utopia.

Citizens of other countries should know us much better now, and that our present-day Rwanda is far more than a bitter land of death, despair, and genocide. I hope that you are "all fired up" and ready to take whatever actions are necessary to obtain a more brilliant future!

For the young people, I wish you could hear how much my heart shouts for your success. I know you are capable. I know you are willing. I know you love our nation. Dream! Believe! Soar! Do not let anyone or anything stop you. Create the Rwanda you want for your children—and your children's children.

Go ahead; I dare you to build your empires! I dare you to build your hospitals! I dare you to eradicate poverty, discrimination, and all forms of inequality! For seventeen years, our generation has cleared the way for you, so make us proud. Do what we could not do! Leave copious wealth to the future generations of Rwandans, and teach your children to maintain the legacy that you have built.

To our Government and our beloved President Kagame— THANK YOU for your myriad labors and efforts! Thank you for your beliefs and dreams. Thank you for your hard work and dedication. I implore all of you leaders, share your powers; and after you have served well, step down and let others lead. Then take all of your wisdom and lavish it on the new generation. Each of you is so valuable! However, our system is fragile. All the good we have done will only remain as long as we stay true to our cause.

We know the devastation that occurs when we over-control, seek power for ourselves, and are wantonly selfish. We have paid dearly for that—living in an unfathomable genocidal hell. We buried our dead families, rotting in the streets. We destroyed our communities, causing a near deathblow to the nation. It is only by the grace of God that we recovered.

Shall we destroy ourselves again? Shall we allow the nation to suffer at the expense of our own personal gain? God forbid—God forbid this! It will take a unified effort between the citizenship and the leadership to reap what we have sown. We have built unity, trust, forgiveness, and a powerful reconciliation that the rest of the world doesn't understand—yet. We have done something unique and extremely great.

We have given our youth a future—so pass on the torch! We have built up a system of gender equality—don't let it fail! Provide equal opportunities. Provide equal education. Provide equal access. We have made our nation safe with the National Police and our military—don't corrupt it! We have shown our children the way—don't disappoint them!

To the international community: it is deeply engraved in our history how you abandoned us in our hour of utmost need. It is also in our history how you sought our forgiveness, stepped back in, and offered us ample assistance. We appreciate your efforts. But this is our time. We must set our own agenda. We must rise to the occasion. If you truly want to help us, then support our own efforts.

There is a saying in Western cultures, "Give a man a fish and he will eat for a day. Teach a man how to fish, and he will eat for a lifetime." When you give a man a fish he becomes dependent on you. When you teach a man how to fish, he becomes dependent on himself.

This is our time. That is what we are: a nation that's striving and obtaining more independence every day. We are empowering ourselves. We want to be an example to the rest of Africa and the world. Go with us down that road. We can no longer be dependent. Support our independent efforts!

Those in the international community who've never owned up to their support of the horrible events of the past think we will never succeed. We will, in spite of everything! You hold no abject level of importance to our nation. Our future is what is important. The most powerful of all life lessons is that you reap what you sow; as a nation, we have chosen to forgive and move on, but in our history we will never forget.

To our women and girls—SHINE! Hold your heads up! Embrace your new opportunity to prosper. Get involved in leadership; start right there in your own community. Be a voice for the women's movement, and never do anything that would impede that progress.

To our men—love and support your women and daughters. Be the men that our ancestors were, and treat them all like queens and princesses. Be a family man. Be supportive! Grow together as a family. Be part of family planning. Be active in learning about and educating others in safe sexuality. Restore against the emotional damage done to our women during the genocide, as a man of outstanding character and sensitivity; be the shoulder your woman needs to lean on. End domestic violence! Encourage each other's dreams and do big things. Plant a vision for your children.

To our national security, the men and women in uniform (the Army and the police)—thank you for keeping us safe. Thank you for extending our Rwandanism to other nations. Your good works are truly appreciated, both at home and abroad! Never forget your true purpose, and never lose the trust that took so long to build. We love you and truly support you.

To our beloved nation—this is your time!

Who am I that I can write this book and present such a charge to the nation? I'm a citizen, just like you! I'm not in politics. I'm not in leadership, and there is no political agenda in this book. I'm someone who has chosen to freely engage in the process of democracy, to do "the greatest good, for the greatest number," and to live a life of allegiance and patriotism to my country. I'm a real-life "mover and shaker" because I've chosen to become only one small part of a much greater system and to use the rights that our Constitution has provided us. Every single citizen of Rwanda has the right to do the things that I've done.

I know one thing for sure: this won't be my last book. There is vast and innovative change going on in my country and in the world. Stay tuned, and you'll see a lot more about what our Rwanda and all of its courageous, innovative and patriotic citizens can do.

But—what can *you* do?

Write your books! Create your dreams! Live successful, productive, and joyful lives! These are rewards for the many years of suffering and hard efforts by our dedicated citizens and beloved leaders. I have a great deal more to say. What do you say, Rwanda—what do you want to do?

This is now and forever your time!